SIMULACRA

FIRST EDITION
Copyright 2024 © by J. Shannon Webster
ISBN: 979-8-9881271-0-9

Library of Congress Control Number: 2024920115

Cover Design: Lauren Hill
Interior Design: Nathan Brown

MEZCALITA PRESS, LLC
Norman, Oklahoma

SIMULACRA

100 Poems

J. Shannon Webster

Table of Contents

Acknowledgements

Thanks to:

Nathan Brown, Lou Ann Webster,
and Hannah Webster for the title

STM Team: Lander Bethel, Jeff Finch,
Gene Harbaugh, Roger Harwerth,
Sam Lanham, Howell Martin, Beaux Lewis,
Matt Miles, Neill Morgan, Drew Travis

Highland Avenue Poets: Barry Marks,
Mel Campbell, Roger Carlisle,
Steve Coleman, James Ferguson,
Tom Gordon, Chervis Isom, Charles Kinnaird
Matthew Layne, Ed Wilson, Michael Yusko,
Nick Gaede

Jemez Springs Poets: Margaia Forcier-Call,
Anita Punla, Stan Renfro, James Cooper

SIMULACRA

MEZCALITA PRESS

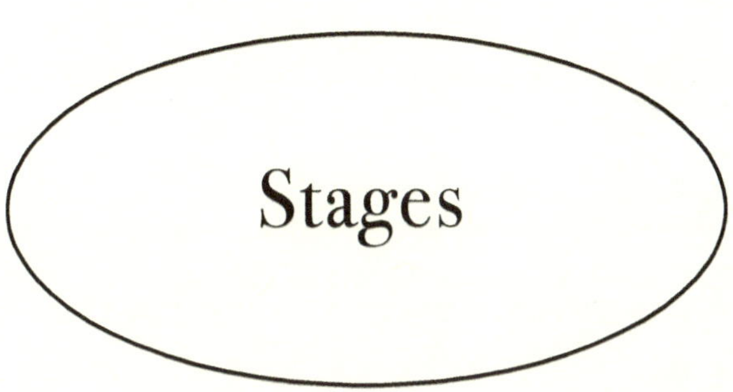

First car — $500
Transmission packed with sawdust
But it *was* purple

Privateers

There are no greater allies
            than the aged and the young.
I'm seventy, he's five, and
            for now we're both alive
at the same time and what a time
            it is we're having!
Son of my son, bright and brave,
            from his deck
we skim the wave
            of the wind-tossed Carib,
and we call our ship *The Raven*.

Merlin to his Arthur, I'm Chewbacca
            to his Solo,
he for now my catechumen,
            Robin Hoods upon the sea.
Plastic sabers clack, we sail
            the back yard into glory
and gain a lasting treasure,
            a subtle one to measure:
he creates, he intuits that what matters is the story.

The Raven is a fast ship,
            not weighed down with heavy guns –
a Corsair trim and low,
            made deliberate for boarding.
Sun and cookies, watermelon,
            for training it's an ideal place
to learn what counts – love and valor, honor is
            its own reward, and some things are
more important than the washing of your face.

Others are charged to guide his mind,
        but I mean to shape his heart.
The young more recent come from God,
        the elder on a reach for home,
from places on the edges can see
        each other as a sign.

It's a natural alliance, the old man, the grandson.
        I help him banish monsters;
perhaps someday he'll help with mine.

They despise us, call us Pirates,
        but we favor "Privateers,"
fighting kings and mercantilers
        from the shadow of the poor.
When hope pines for a sigil
        but no sign of one is found,
lift your eyes to the horizon,
        see the dark hull of *The Raven*,
standing off Barbados in the dawn.

Cibola

Away to the ships, lad, away!
Put behind the life of the fold.
Mundanity fades with the receding coastline.
Ahead lie Cibola, Xanadu and Shambhala.

Flee, or be forever digging potatoes on the croft,
Or eight hours affixing whopadums to ferglenobs,
Ere you be lost in the quarterly earnings report,
Or find yourself cutting grass at Country Clubs.

Dare the unknown shore, the march up country.
Follow the likes of Xenophon, Polo, Bulba, and
Drake, Narbona, Cochise and d'Artagnan.
Let Zorro, Kirk, and Baggins be your guides!

Leave the hearth and do not return
'Til you have a tale worth telling.
Do not seek it only in your dreams and linger,
While it shapes you more than drudgery does.

Hear me now, Tigger knew things Eeyore did not.
It is Possibility, not Conformity, shapes Faith.
For each day the light of the rising sun
Shines down on a glittering world.

May the story you hear as you go to your bed
Be as far from routine as it rings.
It's an old man's job to broaden the map
and corrupt the children with dreams.

At 15 Months
(to a grandchild)

You hold aloft
      in wonder, your treasure,
      beaming at
            an ear of corn.

You do not yet know
      that pain is coming,
      that disappointment lurks
            in your friend's motives,
            and your lover's,
      that the world will hurt you.
            Often.

You do not yet know
      the dark that will infest you
      and someday break
            your father's heart.

But he knows. He remembers.
      It is why
            he cares so much,
            loves so much,
            and is such
         a good, good man.

It is why, secretly,
      he is afraid.

Fortune Cookie

You will enjoy doing something different this weekend.

Well, that is a reasonably safe forecast.
With age I have become more tractable.
Change or stasis, one as good as the last.

I've fewer opinions, more lightly held
(with requisite obvious exceptions).
Sometime ago my darker moods dispelled.

Had I died young, they'd have said, "What an ass!"
and would not have been wrong in that measure.
But tide and sand have ways to polish glass.

Each day I wake to a world renewed –
the sun brighter, the rain more fresh,
and am staggered dumb with gratitude.

Can you name a place from which is sundered
song, color, touch, sweet scent of being?
I walk, a mendicant among wonders.

Letting Go

It is the season of relinquishment
        of stopping, letting go.
The baton is lowered;
        the last instrument case closes.
Ledgers return to folios,
        monitors go dark.
Lesson plans are filed away,
        lunch boxes close for the last time.
No lab report prints out,
        nor law demands redress.
No Bible opens, no saw reciprocates;
        it is the season of relinquishment.

The alarm does not rouse the sleeper,
        the calendar lists no rite to attend.
No vessel languishes at dock, waiting;
        rails and runways lie bare,
Lifts and limos afford no transport;
        there is nowhere to be.
The page lies vacant;
        obligation is in retreat.
No rule but liberty maintains,
        and lasting room for wonder.
It is the time of letting go;
        the season of relinquishment.

Life Plans

Winter is harder these days.
The chill gets deep into my bones.
I no longer hear well, and something
is wrong in my gut.
The pain in my hands though,
a constant companion,
reminds me I am alive.
I am still here, in the house
we built with younger hands.

My friend down in the city,
losing sight and capacity,
lives now in one of those
obliquely named retirement homes.
"Senior Living', they call it.
Or is it "Senior Dying"?
When I look at the faces and the
aggressively unremarkable décor,
I contract sadness.

Don't let that be my last stop.
Let me egress on no whimper, but
a crescendo. A death worthy of
stories to great grandchildren.
A fair fight with a wolf, perhaps,
while holding a bottle of single malt.
Bears are omnivores, eat anything –
nuts and berries, Snickers wrappers,
small animals, even a Presbyterian.

But no hurry. I am far from done.

Mesas rise above like transept and spire,
the scent of pine on the wind my incense,
the world around my cathedral, and
in it with me my lovely life-companion.
It probably doesn't get better than this;
all is sacrament, all is well. I am thankful.
Yet sometimes, on the painful days,
I smell bears.

The Starbucks Chronicles:

I

I could read her like a book
if she was written all in braille…
starting with my fingertips
in the thick, dark tresses
at the top of her head,
to feel every line down
her spine in that backless dress.

At my table I can almost feel the texture
of her caramel macchiato skin.
As though she can read me from afar, she turns
in line, looks, and leafs through my thoughts.
Is this how romance stories go?
This is novel – nothing for which I have
reference. Am I creating fictions for my ego?

She is served, she pays, and carries her
cinnamon latte toward the door.
Her every movement is poetry, and I can't
even summon a "Morning" as she passes by,
trailing the scent of papyrus,
and lost words.
She is a mystery.

II

I shouldn't bring my laptop in here.
And I shouldn't get in online fights

with stupid Quora trolls.
The topic is gun safety laws.

"I can own," he writes, "as many AR-15s
as I want, and the government has
nothing to say about it. 2nd Amendment!
They can't tell me what to do!"

I type his name in the search bar
and look him up on Facebook.
Lovely man; has that Junior Samples thing
going for him. Sigh.

How old are you? Of course "they" can.
Have you ever actually read the Constitution?
Or the applicable laws? Or how about
Steinbeck's *Of Mice and Men?*

Read that, especially the part
about Lennie and the puppy,
then get back to me. And oh yeah,
Grow up. You have too many toys.

III

Why do old men cry so much?
That's me in the corner –
the oldest hippie in the coffee shop.
Okay, the only hippie,
sitting with a Venti Americano,
whatever the hell that is.
(Coffee, I hope.)

Some customers come and go.
Others stay and…do what they do.
Most are looking at tablets.
Screen people. I can't tell if
they're reading or on social media.
I hope they are reading – books or
whatever. Anything else is crap.

I still like the feel of paper, hardbound.
The oldest person in room is identified
not just by tears but by the book,
which cover I cannot hide.

Fear and Loathing in Las Vegas.
Hunter Thompson. There was a time
this was not a geezer book, but raised
eyebrows and BP's.

This is why old men cry:
    a)   to make up for when
        we were not allowed.
    b)   in 1969 we had hope, and lost it.
    c)   we never learned to make love stay.
        (Sorry Mr. Robbins. We tried;
        We were beaten.)
Sitting in the coffee shop with a tear
rolling down my cheek, I read about having
the right kind of eyes to see
*"the high water mark — that place where
the wave finally broke, and rolled back."*

1942

(on restoring a 1942 Harmony Patrician Archtop)

I was born Southside Chicago in 1942,
and named *Wartime Patrician*
for what we were going through.
I had a rosewood tailpiece because
the steel all went to war.
Then that's what I was making music for.
      Believe, be brave, B7augment2
      That's what we did in 1942

I was built to put out sound,
not meant for dulcet tones,
so I could hold my own with
Big Band saxes and trombones.
As time goes by I played the
 sunny side of Dorsey's Street,
worried how could I compete with that elite?

The next years brought Chuck Berry –
and me and Maybelline and Johnny
tried to be good and play tunes
that we had never seen.
Dylan and Woody made up all those
songs to right the wrong,
and guitars were the tool they built them on.

Then late one night on a Memphis street
I was traded for cocaine,
and sold at a pawn shop
to a boy who never learned to play.
Consigned to a dark garage when

my neck broke off in a drunken fight,
for 30 years I never saw the light.

One night on something called *eBay*
I was bought by some old fool,
who swore he'd make me play again;
he did not know the rules.

He carved a neck, joined a fretboard,
shaved my braces down,
glued me up and sanded me around.

He kept my rosewood tailpiece
and left in my face the scars,
a record of my journey through
the dance halls and the bars.
But I could not make a decent sound
to keep me from disgrace,
and spent three more years living in a case.

The old fool took that case
one night to the lone village saloon,
took me out, strapped me on,
and put my strings in tune.
A fiddle and a bass were there;
my God, they had a band!
I felt the music grow; could I play again?

Yeah, man!
Believe, be brave, B7augment2
Just like we did in 1942.

Curmudgeon's Carol

I should comb
        my hair? Why?
Am I having
        my picture taken?

If I tuck in
        my shirttail
How will I clean
        my glasses?

Yeah, I put on
        white socks
        with black shoes.
It offends your aesthetic.
        But does that
        diminish *you*?

I walk slower
        than you in the Mall.
I seem to be in your way.
        I'm old.
Maybe I know it doesn't help
        to hurry.

I had raspberry pie
        for breakfast.
That's some on my shirt.
I'm saving it
        for later.

Yes; old men cry, a lot.
        We know.

We have learned to feel things
        more deeply.
        Give it a try.

How does this work?

If I clean up,
        walk briskly,
and change
        my sartorial aspect
Do I win a trophy?

Death Valley, CA – November

It's Fall in the high country,
      stream beds are bare,
the pine trees all wear snow in their hair;
      so do I.
The hawk like a thunderbolt
      drops on the hare,
Who lashes a kick out, and dies
      with a glare in his eye.

The hunter that strikes from within
      is not so clean;
It's a twist of the mind; it is sneaky and mean.
      It is doubt
That a life spent in searching out
      matters unseen
Will count much when time all along
      has been running out.

People and places I've blessed
      and I've cussed
I try to write down, but they all
      turn to dust on the page.
Muscle and bone that
      I no longer trust,
memories passing like cloud shadow
      crossing the sage.

The love of companions is
      for its own sake,
but more miles lie between us
      than what I can make in a day.
Finding a new friend is not a bad break,

but you can't make and keep them
as fast as they
take them away.

The touch of a woman,
a bottle of beer,
are not quite enough to
dispel all the fear.
Is it smart to mark the lost chances,
the passing of years,
or worry the patches, the hole
and the tears in my heart?

My back to the corner,
I load up my quill,
there deviled by shades that
refuse to stand still in the light.
I'd off to the high country,
sit on a hill, and wait for the wolf
to come down if he will –
a fair fight.

Up on the ridgeline the short days
are shedding their light.
Death Valley lies down below
in the gathering night.

Becoming an Old Man

I'd like to become an old man.
Having known a lot those,
      I've liked near every one.
To be counted you have to be
      seventy plus some and know
      you could be nearly done.
I'd like to become an old man,
      but not the fearful, angry kind,
      nor the timid nor the sad,
      nor one waiting just to die.
Only an eager year to go,
      to wake up old and glad!
I'd like to become an old man
      no Sixty-Seven GTO
      with mag wheels and decals of fire,
      nor once-plush junkyard Oldsmobile.
No longer driven, but cruising.
Rather a Studebaker with new tires.
I'll become an old man who's made
      friends with himself, who laughs freely
      and is easily amused.
I want to let go and watch
      grandchildren grow, and
      not give a damn when confused.
I'll accrete the eccentric,
      the peculiar, on purpose,
      but don't patronize me; I bite.
My dues are paid, I owe nothing
      to anyone but to run
till they turn out the light.

My Last Dog

At my age, and the way I'm feeling,
       this could be my last dog.
Like me, she is slow to morning,
and cannot descend the outside stair.
       She stands at the top and cries.
At my age, and the way I'm feeling,
       were this not my last dog,
would it be unkind to gain a pup,
if my life may lack the years to equal
       a life lived in dog years?
At my age, and the way I'm feeling,
       were this not my last dog,
an aging dog made sudden homeless
could take some peace in my company,
       and lie beside my fire.
At my age, and the way I'm feeling,
       this could be my last dog,
when the children divvy up my things,
and bankers settle my estate.
       But who would love my dog?
At my age, and the way I'm feeling,
       this could be my last dog,
in a rich, companioned, 7-dog life
of bright eyes, lifted paws, love and trust,
       the first dog to the last.
At my age, and the way I'm feeling,
       this could be my last dog,
and who will I be without her?
Sit, Gracie…stay.
       Please stay.

Grizzled

There in the morning mirror
        grizzle looked back,
        from my face and head to chest.
It must have been there for awhile;
        I didn't notice.
Proof you're grizzled is –
        you don't care.
Age and grizzled are not the same.
You can age without being grizzled,
        but the grizzly have some
        pretty hard miles on them.
Just so, grizzly and grisly are not the same,
        but it could seem so to
        the languid and overly cultivated.
Color and grizzled are not the same.
Webster's defines "grizzled" as
        "gray, graying or speckled."
But we know it is more
        than that, don't we?
More like a condition, even
        a state of being.
For example, I did not start this poem with
        "*When I woke up this morning…*"
(Never do that!)
        and everyone over 60 thinks,
        "*You were on my mind…*"
Not only that, but they hear
        the melody line, perhaps all day.
"You Were On My Mind,"
        We Five, title cut, 1965.

The rest of the album held covers.

It was their only hit. But also
          the first use of electric guitar
          on a Folk album.
We who are grizzled know these things.
Useless information, to be sure, but
          we know other things too.
The grizzled can open your "P-trap"
          in under a minute,
          clean your battery posts, make tools
          from unlikely household items and
          teach children to color outside the lines.
The lines in my face tell the tale,
          and grizzled is more gritty than pretty.
Willie is grizzled, Nolte, Duvall, Jimmy Carter.
          Morgan Freeman and Redgrave.
          Mirren makes it work.
Cuba Gooding and Reba, by contrast,
          are too cute by half for grizzlement.
The grizzled have been around,
          have memory, and resilience.
We, the grizzled, no longer worry much about
          cholesterol, PSA, IRAs, or what you think.
 We are not sitting around waiting
          to die. We are simply
          anticipating what comes next.
Or not. We may be waiting
          for the library to open. Or the pub.
We sure as hell *are* going to die, we just don't
          want to be worrying about it when we do.
It's not like we didn't see it coming.
Do not think we are burned out and jaded.
Rather, we are sanguine and patient.

It won't go well to be dismissive.
The grizzled do not cringe, but
          be careful. We *will* bite you back.
We are not obliged, and
          the truth no longer hurts.
We've already had more time than we'd thought.
Life is a gift. There is no final exam.
Consider grizzlement as a sort of adornment –
          one with advantages.
When three times as many years lie
          behind as could ever be ahead,
          some focus is gained.
We've lost too many fights, too many loves, buried
          too many friends to worry about bullshit.
The grizzled have capacity.
There is time enough and interest left
          for the things that matter.
As much as we've been around, we still
          look to be intrigued.
We're just waiting for the punch line and
          the grace to grizzly bear.

Norwegian Wood
Cruise Ship Dance Floor

A few weeks shy of 70, she stepped out
        onto the hardwood floor because
the cruise ship band was really, really good
        at channeling Roy Orbison.
55 pounds heavier than in 1969,
        her hair dyed a cautious red,
the lines in her face grown deep.

> *Pretty woman, walkin' down the street,*
> *Pretty woman, the kind I'd like to meet,*
> *Pretty woman, walk my way…   ~Roy Orbison*

But her feet and her hips remembered,
        with every sure step and reach,
what it meant to be 19,
        when her moves made young men yearn.
Tonight when she danced
        everybody knew that.

∫∫∫

12 years old, she looked younger;
        whatever afflicted her in gestation
contorted her mind and her body,
        and so short, so short. The pink raincoat
her sister gave her nearly touching ground;
        she lurched randomly on the hardwood,
to no particular beat.

> *What's goin' on on the floor? I love this record,*
> *But I can't see straight anymore.*

She did her best to copy the moves and motions
        of sister and the other dancers.
Her face shone with delight, her smile with glee,
        and those who saw her felt
their own hearts rise in their chests
        and dance with joy.

♪♪♪

Tall and lean, he was an okay-looking guy
        who wouldn't see 50 again.
The band had finished their set; the dance floor
        cleared and the house music came on.
He moved alone onto the floor,
        right hand on his abdomen,
self-aware but not self-conscious.

If you said this life ain't good enough,
I would give my world to lift you up.
Because you're so smooth…   ~Rob Thomas

A graceful shuffle, he glided the hardwood alone and
        who knows what he thought of?
Anita before the divorce? Linda before the cancer?
        Perhaps he was simply wondering –
"Whatever became of people dancing in pairs?"
        Those who watched that poignant journey
moved with him.

May I have the next dance?   Anybody?

Cemetery Cleanup Day

Chain saws snarled, weedwhackers
 made rattlesnake sounds.
Cleanup day at the church cemetery.
Thigh-high grass fell in golden sheaves.

Branches of juniper and piñon pine,
by consensus dead or unseemly,
fell from their perches to be carted
to the slash pit in five truckloads.

Gravestones and monuments, for the
first time in seasons, shook off their
torpor in the newfound sun, to stand
as straight as their years allowed.

Laid out in 1875 by founding minister
Rev. John Shields – he stated a condition
that no future cemetery headstone
would be taller than his.

The cemetery is populated with
passed-on Presbyterians, also
people of the parish and tribal lands.
We connect through faith and soil.

Each plot I worked, if not too eroded,
I read out loud, caught by compulsion
to honor the names
 of Saints long silenced.

ELEANOR MOORE
NOV.2.1930 <> JUNE 23.1971
WE LOVE YOU

Eleanor Beloved, you died the same age
I had a heart attack. We have that in common.
And here we both are. One up, one down.
Who can say why you died and I did not?

CHARLES ALBERT
SON OF G.M. AND
CORRINE MAY DIED
AUG. 20. 1923.
AGE 1 Yr * 5 MO.S 20 DAYS

Charles, there was no room left on the
gravestone. Had there been, I trust
your parents would have added not
only the hour, but the very minute.

BELLE A.
WIFE of the Rev. J.M. SHIELDS
DIED MAR. 29 . 1900
IN HER 39TH YEAR

Belle, it is a shame your marker honors you
only as someone's wife. Those frontier days
demanded you be more. I carry a tapeline.
You forever topped him by two inches, Ma'am.

Place

You wouldn't be here
had you not turned up there
to wash up somewhere

Petrichor

The drought was long and deep,
Rendering growing things desiccated,
Shriveled and sere, their colors muted.
Juniper and spruce dropped needles,
Yuccas groaned in the hot stillness.

Until clouds came dark and fulsome,
Carrying wet scent of a west wind freshening.
Piñon pines lifted their crowns to the rain,
Keening throughout the forest as if they
Could, would, stretch their limbs to reach.

Chipmunks and other small ones rose
From burrows below, come from hiding
To lift their dusty faces and attend.
New rain fell on hot rock and dirt, then
Came a smell – earthy, mineral and clean.

All creation breathed in primal aroma as
Limestone mated with the blood of gods.
Geosmin flooded our heads and hearts,
Like when you've been long away,
And come home.

King On the Mountain

The Chevy truck winds through its gears,
climbing out of the caldera toward 10,000 feet.
Cloud cover falls behind, below, and brilliant sun
breaks through over Spruce and Ponderosa pine.
As if some hidden hand threw a switch,
aspens alert with a startling vivid yellow.

I slam on the brakes just in time, and hear
everything on the jump seat hit the floorboard.
Onto the road and across it four juvenile elk trot
gangly, curious and innocent, no care in the world.
Two skittish cow elk follow, anxious at my presence,
so close I can almost reach out and touch them.

Next, he processes slow, a huge bull carrying a rack
with so many points I cannot quickly count them.
The antlers of his crown reach to heaven.
He pauses long, then continues the noble march
he must have done at his coronation, head turned
to watch me eye to eye – defying me to separate him
from his charges.
The pickup purrs at idle;

"I would not dream of it, Sir."

Snow

Snow falls like hunger
On my dry mountain acre,
Covering my world with
A gentle white pallor,
Occupying the opulent pines,
The deck, the cabin roof.

All terrain is altered by
The constant gentle caress
Of snow. Rock's edges built
Into heaped, pale hummocks
Enveloping, inviting investigation
Of the mystery beneath.

Pristine overlay kisses earth,
Altering what was there.
I lie down in softness, sweeping
Over me a quilt of crystals.
My body is bathed in beauty –
But cold, oh so cold.

San Juan County, 1968

We could see the flames
throwing light like a mirror-ball
against the sandstone cliffs of the mesa.
From our parking spot at the airport
across the valley,
we watched the city landfill
burning in the desert night.

On the hood of the Oldsmobile
Thomas played his guitar, always
singing songs to Sarah.
In the back seat,
Mark popped open a 3.2 Coors
we'd bought in Durango,
and passed a cool can up to me.

I took it in my left,
lifted from the wheel's necker-knob,
my right hand trapped
in the sleeve of Kristi's t-shirt,
where I was allowed to access
the top of her breast, never the nipple –
sitting easy with the sweating beer,
and Kristi's sweat now, too,
in the desert night.

From our parking spot at the airport
across the valley,
we watched the lights
of fire trucks heading out
in a line like red ants.
Next week we'll light it again.

People Have Their Ups and Downs

I stand 10 inches from the cliff edge
yet secure on solid stone. Beyond that…
a bit of an overhang, then the rock face
is fractured but sheer, 850 feet down to water.
7,000 feet up, at the Rio Grande Gorge
near Taos, the air is thin, crystalline.
I can see forever from here.
The landscape is breath-taking.

More than 125 jumpers have died
off the Gorge bridge – 5 or 6 a year.
Less than Niagara or the Golden Gate,
more than the Empire State building.
People have their ups and downs.
When they are down they want to be up
and some go up, on bridges, buildings, cliffs,
to transit back down as fatally as possible.

This view is gorgeous, breathtaking.
Not so breathtaking as impact,
but it lasts far longer. It is heartrending
that some cannot see forever from here.
At the edge, only a discrete millimeter
delimits continuing and not continuing,
being and not being,
up and down.

Rio Rancho Grass

An Orison to the
Intercessor of the Suburbs

*

Thank you, St. Marvin, for:
bringing us forth onto desert arid and pristine,
blessing carpets of alien grass verdant green,
even as we brought the water table low;

and for allowing us, where it did not flourish,
to envelop transformed ground with hues garish –
crushed rock from the sacred quarry.
Let grassy lawns be flattened down,
and neighbors meet on even ground.

*

Grateful are we, St. Marvin, for grass, and
concession that we might spread wide across the land
without forethought, constraint or benefit of plan,
or pointless "city center," for

houses identical save slight color variance,
so closely built that proximity and appearance
may foster in us a sense of community.
Sans belonging, random catchments
may form passable attachments.

*

Bless you, St. Marvin for:
granting our landfill be sited near the high school,
that our young have convenience of place as a tool
for discarding their paraphernalia.
For advent of Staples, Kohl's, McDonalds, Best Buy,
Home Depot, Walmart, Starbuck's
and Tractor Supply –
bringing the world to us, Intel inside.
Be Intel our refectory,
Sub-divisions our rectory.

*

Estimable Marvin grant us
wall-sized TV's for our sofas,
teams to cheer on,
from schools we never went to
in towns we've never known,
and bourbon to anaesthetize our doubt.

Bless to us our grilling outside on summer nights,
o'er the river far from Albuquerque's troubled lights
and the sound of sirens.
As always, thank you for the grass,
and more than a little weed.

Trout

My people swam in the deepest part
below the surface of convention,
away from the liminal boundary marking the air.
If referenced in these days at all,
        it's tales around the fire
         of wild things seldom mentioned.

And I am one as well.
The current brings me daily bread
if I'm still or cast the waters.
        Dark above and pale below, and
        by the time you mark the flash I've sped.
Flowing 'round the stones and bends
in angry froth to standing pool,
to carom from the mountains –
        but in cascade or eddy
           only vary cold to cool.

If by mistake I take the lure,
to throw the hook, I'm strong enough.
    To break the line, I'm long enough
        to muscle sleekly through the riffles,
        still there,
              upstream somewhere,
                in the deepest part.

The River Runs

Mayfly copy on a gossamer thread,
Arcs for the bend in the stream.
Caddis in riffles calls to the spotted
Leprechaun deep in the seam, who
Eager strikes, fights, cedes not the least,
And is, in the space of damn or redeem,
Netted, admired and released.

The South Platte

West of Denver,
East of the Divide,
cross the North Fork
of the South Platte –

a stream so rapid
cold and clean
to behold it makes
you feel forgiven.

Clear ice but a fortnight past
has become melt-water
consecrating new needles,
bright on Ponderosa pine.

Kenosha pass at 10,000 feet,
and the headwaters yet
gleam transcendent
in thin mountain air.

Now the west face slopes low
into blessing, a vast bowl
of spring graze for horses
and herds of neighboring elk.

Douglas Firs stand close
to break the winds of April.
Roofs pitched steep will shed
snowfall still to show.

Here is beauty born of
isolation, life ransomed

from lean flanks
of hardship and commitment.

A dark and lonesome cabin,
spare of adornment,
is shaped to lines as exacting
as Calvin's God.

The descent reaches level at the
road bend. A painted trailer
pushes "Pony Rides/$30 Hour."
Turn away, toward the high country.

Transaction, Chichicastenango

My bride and I and our Best Man,
J.R., sat sunning on the flat top
of our small hotel on market day.

Stretched below, roofs of red clay
traced the valley where the town lay
shadowed by Cerro Pocojil.

A small, dark woman with cracked heels,
broadened feet and a great straw basket
bore her wares through the courtyard arch,

which brought the manager to march
out yelling and chase her away.
Before long, she edged in again.

She set down her basket, reached in
and lifted on her arm a blue blanket.
She held up all ten fingers – the price.

J.R. raised four, a move to entice.
She pointed to the beige design,
smiled, and held up four on each hand.

Our man came back with five and a grin,
and when the price fell to seven
got up, went in and went down.

He returned after cash went round,
displaying his purchase. We grumped,
"There are no camels in Guatemala!

No camels, J.R., not even a llama!
How much did you finally give for that?"
The Best Man raised his blanket high,

tilted his face back to the sky:
and laughed at his own jubilant cry...
"Fifteen!"

Penn Station

(for Bob Dylan and François Villon, a Ballade)

Where coming and going is all the norm,
Doesn't "Terminal" seem like a strange name?
Me and Buck and Jilly Bird fled the storm,
Going down there with others doing the same.
Warm is the only reason why we came;
Ain't got no other sort of base intent.
Even if your last dollar has been spent,
Keep your head up, but leave your eyes down low.
Pride is the only price you pay for rent.
It's a cold world; there's no place else to go.

"Cop coming through," someone gave the alarm.
"All of you strays ought to try and look tame."
Jilly hid the track marks on her arm.
Buck took a last drag and put out the flame.
The buggers at the top have rigged the game;
It was by design, and that's how it went.
Who's got the money is who owns the mint,
So look up at the view, enjoy the show.
There's nothing got this way by accident.
It's their world, and there's no place else to go.

Most don't mean anyone personal harm,
And most days there ain't nobody to blame.
Buck's short on smart, Jilly's short on charm,
But the very most pointless feeling's shame.
"It's God who's at fault here", many will claim.
God said, "What did *I* do? To what extent?
You know not everything is heaven-sent.
It's really anybody's game to throw."

There don't seem much percentage to 'Repent!'
It's an odd world, with no place else to go.

Envoi:
Buck said he's been to Heaven, one weekend,
And been through Hell – nothing down below.
You and me and Jilly know what he meant.
There's just one world. There's no place else to go.

Things in Boxes

I wear my father's socks, sparingly and on occasion.
They are patterned with tartaned Scottish terriers,
and he wore them to remember his Donald, as I do
to remember him, over these years. Things matter.
They reify places, times and people who
 made us who we are.

Moving day, and the house echoes emptiness as
things go into boxes. Clean and uncurtained windows
admit light that accomplishes no purpose.
There is little to see. Only the vanishing of things.
As things go into boxes, they lose their place.
The house loses its idiosyncratic character. It empties
and something is lost. The house is at once larger and
reduced. It is a disappearing painting, a blank canvas,
the empty palate for unknown others.

Things have had bad press in the recent era, as though
our sins of acquisition were innately theirs. Yet the
world is filled with things and I love so many of them.
I write in defense of things, especially as they are
given and received.
Things anchor our remembrance and our past.
Things give our memories somewhere to be.
Things attain the patina of touch and sound and living.

I put things into boxes in the echoing room, and each
is more than itself. At a certain point, the things going
into boxes have face and story behind them. These will
travel with us and be brought to light in another place.
Things which have no face or story are piled aside to be
given away. I pack my father's socks.

A sweater I gave Her our first Christmas became
only hanging threads, now somehow made into a pillow.
The world is filled with things
and there is no sacrament
without them, be they simple water, bread and wine.

There are things that hold the presence of another –
sacraments that vanish now into boxes
until they have a place again.
I used to keep my heart in a box,
until She took it out
and gave it somewhere to live.

Bucksnort, Tennessee

*A Report to the Most Reverend Bishop Ricardo Toledo
on the State of Affairs in Bucksnort and Only, TN.*

Dear Holy Eminence Toledo:
I write to advise you of the life or lack thereof
of the Ste. Vivian's Church in Only, Tennessee.
I been guessing you might need to formally
shut it and sell the property for benevolences.
The church hasn't seen a priest in 30 years,
the building's been near gone near that long.
I just periodic cut the grass and I'm Methodist.
The last member moved to the next town over.
No one lives here now. I can tell you about that too.

There's not much left to Bucksnort either, except
conflicting origin stories about the name.
Even at that it's better off than neighboring
Only – a for-sure Ghost Town since Merrill took up
with Jimmy Rainbarrel and came here. Why,
Bucksnort is ten times the size Only was.

I-40 has a sign and exit for Bucksnort, but allows
no return access. You exit onto the Only Road,
a mile-wide circular byway that is the only
road to intersect the Bucksnort Road.
Rainbarrel is Bucksnort's Town Marshall, and he
occasionally patrols the Only Road on days
when nothing is going on. That is every day.
Once, though, he removed a deflated raccoon,
using his own hands!

There's just a few guys in this town, which

of course makes Merrill the Only girl in Bucksnort
(not of an equine persuasion)
and also the only person of color.
That color is orange.
Flaming hair to ripe peach complexion,
to skin-dyed toe ends from when Jimmy
on accident cut off her nails with the miter saw.

Jimmy had anxiety about Merrill moving in,
due to her forceful hair and general orangeness,
and because he'd never slept with a Catholic.
Though not experienced himself, he confesses
no difference that cannot be attributed to that
mass of passionate tangerine hair.

Jimmy and Merrill live on the hillside next over
to Bucksnort Mayor Claude Debussy.
Claude lives with his mother, who as a somewhat
dessicated old crow from Holladay, TN, therefore
does not count as the only or Only girl in town.
Mom Debussy does obtain to a wicked humor
and a bad mouth, which accounts for the day she
acquired a stray cat and named him Clawed.
She'll get out in the yard and call for one or
the other, but nobody knows, not even Claude.
Or Clawed.

Jimmy Rainbarrel is something of a musician,
playing both Banjo and Bowed Psaltery as he does,
so he knew the real Claude Debussy had been a
famous musician of some kind or another.
Jimmy and Merrill will wait outside until

Claude comes out his house, then they'll sing:
"O say Debussy" to the tune of the national anthem.
Claude doesn't like it much. Clawed neither.
But Claude doesn't get mad on account of his
huge crush on the Only girl in Bucksnort.

He set out to lure Merrill away from Rainbarrel,
offering her a position, well several, and
a small stipend to go with it. Merrill was not fooled,
but she had never had a position before.
She asked, "What position?"
Debussy fussed around to come up with Adjutant.
There weren't no work of course, 'cept you know.
Adjutant sounded good to Merrill.

A mad Jimmy went next door to arrest Debussy,
Jimmy being Sherriff and all. They all forgot
that Claude was the Mayor, and he fired Jimmy.
Jimmy couldn't arrest him then,
but weren't nobody happy.

Rainbarrel has a canoe what he rarely uses,
being as how he can't swim and doesn't care much
for water. He only took it out when the creek was low.
So the bottom was rock-scratched all to hell.
Setting in the Adjutant's office adjusting her blouse,
Merrill had an idea, and met him when he came back
with a more-broke boat.

Jimmy has a horse – Whinny, a white thoroughbred.
Merrill put Whinny's reins through the front thwart,
and that horse, she drug Jimmy in that canoe through

the Milo fields and rich dirt of center Tennessee
like a NASCAR champion with a paddle.
Claude watched that beautiful horse on parade,
while knowing Merrill was tired of being Adjutant.

It was later that night that Jimmy found Claude
in his barn, Whinny's stall, case in point,
less than half-dressed and carrying a curry comb.
Claude looked at Jimmy and said, "You're rehired."
And being as how Whinny seemed to be pleased…
In the end, Claude (as Mayor) officiated the wedding
where the bride became Merrill Rainbarrel,
a title she liked because it rhymed so nicely.
(Claude Debussy became quite the equestrian.)
Six Rainbarrel offspring come from that union,
doubling the population of the town, and ensuring
Merrill is no longer the, well, Only girl in Bucksnort.

And that, Most Holy Eminence Toledo, is my report
on the state of affairs… well,
Only in Bucksnort, Tennessee.

Sincerely,
Wesley's Yard Services

Short-Handed at the IHOP

I hesitated to be seated.
I could see at the kitchen window
18 plates poised for pick-up,
lovely and waiting to be served.

They were an affront somehow,
sitting there cooling
just out of reach.
Not because of managerial ineptitude.
Not because it forecast
the service would be slow (it was).

But because it took me back
to high school,
and all those girls who
were never going out with me.

Texas 1957

I was five, it was a magic time.
Dad would stop at a five and dime,
the mercantile on Manchaca Road
before driving home to the ranch.

Dad talked livestock, tools or weather
with men made of tobacco and leather.
He'd buy me a gumball or Tootsie Roll
and one time a bright blue squirt gun.

A mechanical horse I could barely climb
stood up front, and I'd pretend he's mine,
while men's voices talked laws and votes
until they came upon conclusions.

There Dad showed me to a tall, tall man
who patted my head with a giant hand,
while his head held up a giant gray hat.
We left the mercantile for the car.

"We get home, feed the chickens." He smiled.
 Drove and stayed real quiet for awhile,
then said it wouldn't surprise him to see
that Lyndon 'come President someday.

Where Heaven Is

If you would know where heaven is,
        tear the loaf, breathe in…
food of ancients in flour, water, and yeast.
        Labor; bring home bread, its aroma
a feast unto itself. Baked, hot and soft,
        in the oven reliably transmogrified,
smelling of heaven, and heaven of bread.
        See it liquefy butter! Pass the bread.

If you would know where heaven is,
        see the barkeep, tap handles dancing
to the familiar hand's practiced ease.
        The alewife bears a tray of smoky meat
and cheese, and smiling lays it down.
        Barry tunes a bouzouki to Mary's fiddle,
and just listen! For two hours' gravid interval
        heaven sounds, as notes pass ringing by.

If you would know where heaven is
        and baptize weary eyes with grace,
bid relation by the poet, not the priest –
        of the day she walked in lavender,
the sun yet east and dripping glory on the
        field where she wore lavender.
 As heaven closes, so she'll draw near, each
        passing moment mutable with light.

Body Politic

A flutter of wings
then quail eggs break underfoot
Who is responsible?

Albion Alone

To keep us out, Romans built a northern wall.
We let it stand so that we might wall them in.
A part stands still, sign that those who came after
       dealt us so much worse.

We fought their, *their*, bloody wars for Royal gain
until spent, they pulled back to the island home.
"God save the Queen," they sing yet across the earth.
       We might ask, "From what?"

With an Angle of her own – greed and snob'ry,
nostalgic now for pounds, she leaves the union.
But *we* still have friends in Holland, Spain and France.
       Brexit your own arse.

The Warrior in Autumn

Gone from the hearth is the foe, for now.
Sword and buckler hang above the fire.
I fought him long, but for this season
      others lie within his line of march.

I am grown tired with age; little fight is in me.
Winter is but weeks away.
Old wounds and scars ache deep
to the bite of the wind.
      The song of repairs rings from
      hammer and boards,
and the blackened croft can wait
until Spring for seed.

The Great Dissembler is not defeated.
I see him on my television.
      His red-helmed minions laugh and bellow
      their hateful chants.

Wrapped richly in his ego, and at
the bidding of Lords and Moguls,
he targets the helpless among us –
      the poor, the forgotten, the dis-homed.
When the pursed lips in his great, girlie face
      simper and spew hate and lies,
      his sycophants take up the chorus
      and people die.

My blade-arm twitches at the sound of his voice,
as sword and buckler gleam in the firelight.

Ship of Fools

We sail the rising ocean, here
        on Plato's "ship of fools" –
        a leaking scow loose in the stays,
        a crew that has no rules.
Our officers can't navigate
        or steer, or read the wind;
        so those few trained and best equipped
        are never in command.
There's a sorry clown at tiller.
        Was there another choice?
        Our Captain is no sailor, but
        he has the loudest voice!
Yes the Captain is repugnant,
        the most venal brute afloat,
        with a mind that's made of feathers,
        and the morals of a goat.
O, he struts about the wheelhouse
        (he thinks it makes him tall),
        so Garcia, Bosch and I form
        a mutinous cabal.
"He has no art," I say to them.
        "Who'll take him seriously?"
        "I cannot share your laughter,"
        Garcia says to me.
"His sycophants are everywhere,"
        Bosch groaned, "debauched and dim!
        A festival of ignorance,
        all modeled after him!"
The sinking barge is listing right,
        all warning is ignored.
        The sanest thing to do is throw
        the Captain overboard!

Blood of the Martyrs

I

Collective human memory is in the blood,
some say, and heroes, villains, sainted martyrs,
all must heed the requirements that blood
demands, for what are we but flesh and blood?
When all we do is said and done
it matters little if we are washed in the Blood
of the Lamb, or battle-bathed in blood
with which the streams of history run
with scraped elbow welling blood
to Mother's welcome lap and there to weep,
we crawl for final rest, but lie awake to weep.

II

Who commands, decides, is not the one will weep
for mother's sons who fell at war. And blood
of other nations troubles less. Yet lovers weep
for death-robbed futures, and saints will weep
for all the innocents now become martyrs,
who chose to neither fight nor die nor weep.
Commanders and deciders little weep
ever, nor lie awake when day is done
and wonder on the deeds in their name done.
No artifice makes broken hearts to weep,
no design in the faithful, eyes with tears to run,
but honest will to bear and be till over-run.

III

So it is the tides of history run –
drums play while the war-pipes weep
till all around is martial music run
together. Young and poor at
Flanders and Antietam run

to battle or away, from killing fields of blood —
filled in the low places, and discover in their run-
ning there's no reason more to run.
Can we count the dead as martyrs
if the choice was never theirs? For martyrs
who will bear and be neither charge nor run,
and chose not flight or fight. "Thy will be done,"
they may pray. Then they die and they are done.

IV

Natural or not, or by its own hand done,
Death grants no look back to those we've run
with, no satisfaction or praise of things done.
In real life, when life is over and done
with, no grand postscript shines on who weeps
or cares, whether eulogies are done rightly or
wrongly. The dead care not how it's done.
No gloried sacrifice or hero brave whose blood
will change a thing. It is no shed blood on
hands of deciders when commanders have done.
History alters only when power martyrs
small ones, outrage blooms at the death of martyrs.

V

No carols sung relive the hour Herod martyrs
the Innocents; perhaps the act is not yet done?
Remember Irish children turned to martyrs
at Omagh and Drumcree, those whose martyrs'
cries in dying young made all the deciders run
to tables talking peace? At Wounded Knee were
martyrs made, at Memphis, My Lai and Manhattan,
martyrs whose end untimely made us weep.

We are now memory-changed because we weep.
The sacrifice not be planned, the priest not know.
Blood turned again to saving wine.
Thicker than water, they say, is blood.

Envoi:
At the end all change is paid in blood
that spills from the veins of martyrs.
When the shouting is over, the shelling done
and the last line spoken, the credits will run
with the names of the martyrs. Time to weep.

Look What You Made Me Do

There in the grocery, standing in line,
he turned and backhanded his kid.
He said, "Shut up now, I won't hear you whine.
Just look at what you up and did.
When we're out in public, you leave me no choice.
If you want to grow into a man
I've got to have discipline raising my boys."
He cleaned off the blood from his hand.
The boats that were burning were Vietnamese;
the flames lit the soft Texas night.
Immigrant fisherman down on their knees
hid their faces and wept at the sight.
The others said, "These waters ain't yours to fish.
You don't belong here; and its true –
We can't work your hours or live off your catch
so there wasn't much else we could do."
"We're coming at night in a preemptive strike.
It's a globalized world, so it's true
that you can't just run wild and elect who you like –
it affects all the rest of us too.
The companies here need these natural resources
to keep us in shelter and food.
So when you see our planes or you see our forces
remember it's for your own good."
Maybe the story is not what they claim
when the one with the power
is playing the victim,
turning the tables again. Don't play a
"Look what you made me do" game,
or someone here will die before morning
and somebody will have sinned,
and ain't that a shame.

Clemency

A theologian told me once
he was troubled not a bit
if someone went to prison for
crime they did not commit.
We all are guilty of something,
he intoned.

That premise might be accurate,
but I would turn it round about
like Jesus overturned the tables,
to usher *all* the scoundrels out.
Let my people go,
for God's sake.

Finding Terror

Decades ago now,
the World Trade Towers went down.
Terror came to live in our house.
Terror took up residence
in our minds,
in our hearts,
in our dreams and nightmares,
in our imaginations. Soon we saw it
everywhere.

No one questions that
the first responders were brave
and courageous. It didn't last.
We lost something that day.
Our best self has not prevailed,
our better angels never showed up.
Our actions have been ill-advised –
death by drone,
national aspirations that serve
only the few, and the fragmentation
of our common life
as a people.
Drowned in a sea of
grief and confusion.

Over one hundred seventy years ago
Sir John Franklin's
ship went down,
exploring somewhere unknown
in wild waters,
all hands lost,
searching for the Northwest Passage

through the icy seas
of the Canadian arctic.

Still it lay, secret until today,
perfectly preserved in ice water.
She had settled gently, and sat upright,
her proud bowsprit still pointing
the way ahead,
nothing out of place, resting as if
all was ordinary.
The H.M.S. Terror,
in the dark and the cold,
beneath all we see on the surface.
It lies in the dark.
Waiting.
The Terror.

Witness

a Ghazal

> *"… our generation invented a new literature:*
> *that of testimony.*   *~ Elie Wiesel*

Tragedy comes now every day.
　　　　So always there's a witness.
So lest our very souls are hardened,
　　　　someone must bear witness.

Some are expert, others hostile.
　　　　There's some who need protection.
Testimony helps get history right,
　　　　so swear-in a witness.

Some states, to license marriage,
　　　　ask the signature of others.
What's it mean, why do they care,
　　　　for another pair to witness?

Innocents too often die by those
　　　　we've badged and armed with guns,
Video from body cams are
　　　　a way to wear a witness.

What finally moves us to change,
　　　　to act with intent, to care?
Another mass shooting; cameras roll;
　　　　we share a witness.

Who will testify for the poor,
　　　　the damaged and the silent?

Some knowing seems unbearable,
          but speak up! Be their witness.

Those suffering from evil must
          not just be seen, but carried.
The greatest god and the smallest child,
          both are there to witness.

We praise with awe or damn with scorn
          the ultimacy in things,
And if it drives you to your knees,
          remember – prayer's a witness.

Corroborate, authenticate,
          certify, take note, attest!
We validate each other's lives
          when we declare a witness.

We are proof for one another
          that we lived, that we were here,
that we stood upon the earth,
          that we mattered and dared witness.

Roget's has synonyms enough,
          to cover when your words fail,
That you may not be found witless
          when comes your hour of witness.

Half a House

Half a house, swathed in plastic sheeting,
 sits on a flatbed trailer, no semi attached,
on a strip of frontage forty miles from Albuquerque.

Rooms are visible through the sheeting, also a counter.
The rough frontage stands in for a weigh station,
but no one is there to approve permits today.

Overhead, the mid-day sun has washed the sky of color.
Sagebrush, juniper and red dirt stretch to the horizon.
A lonely road.

Why leave half a house by the highway?
Is someone coming back for it? Is the other half lost?
Did someone not count the cost?

Where are the blueprints? Where are the plans?
Will this hold a revival? Or office for a new casino?
Are we on tribal lands?

Did a couple call it off, and each get half?
"The judge said 50/50 and there it is."
"You take the kitchen. I get the bathroom and den."

It can do little more than weigh down a flatbed.
But it does give new meaning to the word "apartment."
A house divided cannot stand.

If we got word to Washington there was half a house
sitting on a roadside in northern New Mexico,
would the Speaker exclaim, *"That's* where it went"?

What if Alicia?

Dear Great Great Grandfather:

My name is Alicia Reyes. I won't be born for
a hundred years but I'm writing you today.
You'll still have family, and a generation on
the way. We live in a house just off the plaza,
here in Kino Bay. Most people now can follow
heart and head, so we run a bakery; and I make
very good bread.

I guess that I should say what this is all about –
I've been wondering if you're wondering how it
all came out:

Dear Great Great Grandfather, would you be
surprised to know that we still have songs and
stories you wrote long ago? Things were harder
then, we learned in school. Compared to how
we're living now, your time seems so cruel...

When nations sent their young ones off to war.
Death fell from the skies as drones and acid rain;
when those who owned it all still clutched for more,
in an overheated world that writhed in pain, while
hungry children cried; with disease so many died,
poor and disconsolate.

Who could count the time and money spent to
hide another genocide or cataclysmic earth event?
The world had lost the rhyme to life, the rhythm
and the sense. I recall the day I read with pride
the way you and your friends worked so hard

against the dark to bring it to an end.

Dear Great Great Grandfather, when all is done
and said, the air is clear, the water's clean and the
children all are fed. There's room upon the earth
for what can walk, swim, fly or crawl, and when a
person takes another's life, that's the rarest thing of all.

Life is good, there's little that we lack. Some
days we talk to whales, and sometimes they
talk back. I guess we never know the things we
leave ahead, or what they'll say downstream
about us after we are dead.

Dear Great Great Grandfather, I wish that you
could see the gifts your life will leave ahead,
because one of them is me…and know it mattered.

It all matters.
And this is my thanks to you.
                                        Love,
                                        Your Alicia.

He promised to tell
everything he's been thinking
It did not take long

The American Religion

So it has come to this.
The American Religion has swapped
its passion for a pact with power,
its wonder for utility.
It asks of us only accommodation.

It is become a faith expedient,
predicated on end-times.
The American religion bookended Jesus
to a miraculous birth
and a resurrection pass into afterlife.

Gone are the Beatitudes, the parables,
gone a call to servant living,
gone a life poured out for the poor and
humble, "the least of these" and
gone is the love. What happened to the love?

In its place are convictions born in
no gospel but English and German pedantry,
concord with political agendas,
and self-congratulatory beliefs that
no one really cares about, not even God.

How curious – a faith with no content.
The Evangelical cartel has tracked
the wrong god into a corner,
and has no options, nothing left to do
but die.

InCredo

I do not believe in Believing.
What you mean is, "I think," or "It is my opinion."
I don't believe in belief as a pass into heaven
nor that God metes out reward and punishment,
nor that I will someday walk hand-in-paw with Jesus,
nor that virtue very often pays its own way,
nor that guys in the white hats always win.

But I do believe in the worth of the poet's potion –
love, beauty and a 20-year-old single malt.

I do not believe
        help drawn from self-help paperbacks,
I do not think it likely
        the USA is the world's best nation,
I do not believe
        I will be long remembered after I'm gone,
I do not find veracity in
        politicians, preachers, or economists.
I am not persuaded
        there is such a thing as progress;

And yet…belief aside…I am amazed…
by morning light glowing through dewdrop on a leaf,
at the deft, alluring voice of Segovia's guitar,
and the way she looks in sleep as I bring
        her first cup of coffee.

Regarding Prayer

I'm suspicious of prayer.
It seems over-reaching
to go about with a hand out
forever beseeching,
as if God doesn't know what she's doing.

It must surely provoke
some divine irritation
to be constantly badgered
with more supplication,
as though God has nothing better to do.

Memos to the Divine,
as in prayer intercessory,
resemble a shopping
list unnecessary,
imploring, as if God needs reminding.

In the prayer of adoration
we may make a great fuss,
but truth is, that prayer
intends really for us
to remember who's God and who's not.

Confession and gratitude –
Two prayers above others.
But we should pray those to
our sisters and brothers,
and listen as God says, "Finally you get it."

Prayer that Bruises

"I'll pray for you."
How often is that delivered as a threat?
Someone wielding the weapon of
prayer to force change in
> your opinion
> your behavior
> your vote.
A prayer that does not
have at heart your best interest.
Some pray to deliver you from
substances and return you to God,
assuming ability by such petition
> to create such a desire in you,
> alter you unknowing
> or ensure God wants you back.
Has God not been there all along?
When did God retire the field?
Are they praying for you to be
something you are not?
> boring,
> compliant,
> socially acceptable?
This would garner divine approval?
A soul formed from milquetoast?
Where is such a God found?
> not in irascible prophet Jeremiah
> not in obsessive apostle Peter
> nor even in weird John's gospel.
Dare we craft pious-sounding
prayers, having never encountered the
God of storm!
Spare us such prayers!

Do you really want a God who
desires to sand off your edges –
          calm you
          sedate you
          still you?
Would not a preferable God be one
who is not afraid of you?
Grant us the God of the whirlwind,
          whose breath smashes things
          who throws rocks from the cliffs
          calling us out where we fear going.
God who thunders at things as they are
and should not be!
Let us see the God who
          burns the sunset
          rattles the chains
          blows collaborators down
from their high and fancy,
not to mention lucrative, offices.
This world is due a God who
breaks things! Who
          started the fires in Bukowski
          put the snark into Shakespeare
          blew up Thompson's typewriter
who taught Dickinson how to
take the top of her head off.

Food Service

When I sit to Sunday table
I'm not very picky, but
I generally prefer the Presbyterians
and their Service with the food.
The menu never varies –
bread and wine –
and the portions are quite small.
But it is served
with such grace.

Church League

The first pitch was an inside curve.
The second clipped my hat.
That's when I charged the mound to hit
a Baptist with a bat.
Less for sport than for redemption.
We played to ward off shame,
until the Ump, divine-inspired
saw fit to call the game.

(Who knew baseball could be so violent?)

Driving for a layup at a
Lutheran twice my size –
a Forward, standing on my foot,
could not do otherwise.
I limped a mile to Mt. Sinai;
I could not feel my toes.
A Hindu doctor cast my foot;
a nurse looked down her nose.

(Who knew Unitarians could be so judgmental?)

The Methodists were strangely warmed,
for 9-Man Flag in snow.
Predestined Presbyterians
would score on every throw.
We jeered them not, out in the lot,
so badly were they beat.
All rancor left there on the field,
not taken to the street.

(Though earlier we had sore need of a Quaker.)

What if the things we heard in church
were how we play the game?
Fairness, courage, self-control and
the honor of a name?

Ah, sport should bear its own excuse;
the contest wonts no tears.
Then regroup at the pub to meet
the Jesuits for beers.

(The post-game sacrament, holy fermentation.)

If Jesus Had a Dog

What if Jesus had a dog?
There's no such mention in scripture,
but it would be quite a small thing
against the backdrop of incarnation.

But if he did have a dog,
what kind would it be?
And would that tell us anything
of the dog's master?

Literalists would say a Canaan Dog,
an AKC recognized breed,
with desert origins in Palestine
going back to antiquity.

Pietists might naturally choose
a St. Bernard, a substantial dog,
rescuer of the lost and also
conveniently blessed by name.

Aesthetes and filmmakers could
gravitate to the Collie, the
German Shepherd, or Retriever,
simply for profile alone.

Having mentioned shepherds,
and sheep showing up as they will
in parables and examples,
any sheepdog would do.

And would evangelicals extol the
enthusiasms of a Jack Russell terrier?

Or cloistered Nuns imagine the sweet
aspect of the little Pomeranian?

But you and I know different, don't we?
We know he would have had a mutt –
rescued from the roadside where
he and the disciples walked.

Said hypothetical dog was male or female;
let's just say it was female.
She was sick and dirty, mangy too.
Scars told of prior misadventures.

One ear was erect, the other torn floppy.
You could count her ribs by sight, and
she was lacking a leg.
Let's just say it was a hind leg.

He would clean and feed and name her,
Maybe *Caleb*, Hebrew for *dog*. Or *Hesed*,
Hebrew for *compassion*. Let's say *Hesed* –
the book says "Jesus had compassion…"

He would heal her injuries but not the leg;
that would have taken awhile.
What? Did you think it would be immediate?
Healing, real healing, takes time.

He would teach her to fetch when he
whispered in her ear: "Bring, Hesed"
(Not the left ear, which was still floppy,
but the other, so she heard right.)

At the banks of the Jordan he would toss
a stick, and she could usually redeem it.
(The Jordan runs shallow, barely enough
for a proper baptism.)

He would scratch behind her ears
and tell her she was the best,
smartest, most beautiful dog
in the whole world.

And because he said it, and
dogs being who they are
and having such huge hearts,
it would be true.

Philosophy 101

It starts with epistemology –
how do you know you know what you know?
The solipsist makes no apology,
asserting the self alone is quantum,
and Immanuel Kant but Genghis Kahn
and therein lies a problem.

Cogito ergo Descartes est.
Words and hours have been squandered
on whether reality exists,
but if we wait around a bit,
conspiracy theorists will show up.
They really love solipsist shit.

Rational, material, ideal,
metaphysical, and do we care
so long as the thing itself is real?
Per another great philosopher,
"It's still not weird enough for me."[1]
So take another offer.

It is worth spending more time here,
if the world is less idea than place.
So pull up a chair, sit down there,
and let me tell you where it starts –
this tavern, *this* beer, *that* young cowboy
on stage singing out his heart.

---

[1] Thompson, Hunter

The Red Horse

The red mare slipped her bridle
in the lot of the *Beer and There*,
and fled at speed in the deepening
dusk of the Arizona night.
Hands from different outfits combed
through cholla, sage and yucca
just to shrug, and go back to the
bar for another beer.

Too young to drink legal, Josefina,
a *Tohona O'odam* beauty queen,
had all her drinks bought for her
at the drop of a cowboy hat.
Coming on ten, Jake busted back in
to scream, "My ride's been stolen!
A droptop blue '67 Malibu.
I restored her myself!"

Ranch hands turned out once again
on the dirt roads and the blacktop,
to later roll back in without a sighting.
"Sheriff 'll get her sure," they said,
"likely enough with a traffic stop."
They settled down for another round.
But the Chevy was never found.
Josefina never made it home.

Around dawn, in the ranch house yard,
the red horse showed up.

Simulacra

Her first trip outside Pennsylvania,
Natalie found a mounted Jackalope
at a curio shop in Tucumcari, and
fixated on that whimsical invention
of an imaginative taxidermist.

No cute bunny, the genuine Jackrabbit
(christened by Mark Twain for its mule ears)
is a long-eared, rangy, gangly hare,
angular of head, calculating of eye.
Natalie's acquisition sported horns
that once belonged to an antelope.

When in later years she'd tell the story,
she'd come to believe she saw one
in the high desert near Santa Fe.
Can we tell a fiction so often we own it
true, or even become the main actor
in someone else's story?

We tell to children myths and tales
of dragons, sorcerers and elves,
for moral formation or to broaden a world.
But draw… what … from a disfigured hare?
From a living room mantle in Nazareth,
 a Jackalope looks at Natalie with critical eye.

Stories mark our place in the world –
we are not so distinct from the tale.
They warn, remember, keep us alive,
and we are shaped by our bravest dreams.

If we are the stories we tell, should they not
be worthy of us, and we of them?
Of the days we pulled from the stone a sword,
walked on water, and wrestled God to a draw
all for the sake of a blessing?

Taxidermy

I lift heavy-lidded eyes
to the mantel above the wide-screen TV,
where Red Fox and Turkey
stand poised in perpetual conflict.
       They watch each other warily
       through glass eyes.

Truth is, they no longer
have a care in the world.
Not like me,
rendered inert by waxing worries,
compound cares,
and a surfeit of stress.

Add to that too little sleep.
too many calories,
and too much alcohol.
       Torpor takes over.
       I'm stuffed.

O Wine

I took my wine last night in clay,
          a sort of coarse goblet, fun,
          a rough-hewn imitation of authenticity.
I have several of those chalices, cups, vessels
          of pottery rough and smooth
          ceramic and stoneware.

Yet something is lost if you cannot
          see the wine.
Like making love with the light off.
Something sensory is missing –
          the intimacy of vulnerability
          exposed, the subject of longing that
          need not be imagined.

But in its glass, almost illuminated,
          the wine waits, open to encounter.
In the goblet, an arched bowl voluptuous as
          a woman's hip.

O wine, you have many names –
          Oinos, Vin, Vino, Yayin, Wine.
O wine, your very names are sensuous:
          Sauterne, Nero D'avola, Tempranillo,
          Zinfandel, Petit Sirah, Pinot Noir,
          Albarino, Fume Blanc, Viogner,
          Gamay, Carmenere, Retsina,
          Madeira, Dolcetto, Semillon…

In the days Jesuits brought their harsh gospel
          to a wineless world, and sent request to
          Rome for advice on Holy Communion.

Word came back that in every land and among
        every people was made a drink that
        "maketh glad the human heart."
That is, it contained alcohol; for good or for ill
a changed and elevated spirit the sole requisite.

Perhaps there must be some danger.
O wine, you can be so bad.
Witness the wino in the alley, lips pressed
        desperately to his Mad Dog as if
        it were a willing hooker.

O wine, you can be so good.
Lifted by glass, you are as kissing
        a lover, transporting heart and mind
        beyond self, in celebration of the other,
        the world and all that transcends.

So the glass lifts, the celebrant tastes
        grape, sunlight, fresh rain, and leaves.
It lingers on the tongue – the terroir, earthy
        and at the end perhaps lingering chalk,
        minerals from below in the soil.
From tongue it travels to inmost being,
        flows pulp-sweet –
        the bitter skin,
        flint and blood,
        sacrifice and sacrament.

Piper Unseen

A piper skirls in my mountain valley,
            far off somewhere.
My neighbor thinks I've conjured him up
            solely from a desire for there to be
            a piper in the valley.
She knows my hearing is not good
            and by rights I should be the *last* to hear
            by any chance an unseen piper.

Yet ofttimes I hear him faint
            in the wee hours dark gray.
Sound carries in the mountains so
            I know him to be far off,
            those mornings he gives a rendition.
It is just at the edge of hearing, but
            the notes are there sure —
            the reedy constancy of the drones,
            and above them the chanter's air.

Surfacing from sleep I smile, for no good reason,
            to think there is a piper in the valley.
I like the notion of a piper, be he real or not.
I set to thinking there is more to
            our valley and our lives
            than reaches the ear,
            and I wish all my neighbors a piper.

On mornings I hear the mystery, it seems
            the coffee yields more flavor,
            the air is more bracing and clear,
            and anything is possible.

There it is now,
        at the very edge of perception –
            the reedy drones,
                    the chanter's far off
                        grace notes.

A Short History of Waiting

Is the greater part of life
          simply......waiting?
Or does it only seem so?
The alternative – to act –
is laden with
          unknown result.
To wait is more prudent.
Hannah waited untold years
          for Samuel to be born.
Penelope waited twenty years
          for Ulysses to get home.
We waited with Cavafy
          for the Barbarians,
and with Beckett's Didi and Gogo
          in meaningless absurdity.
We waited with Ferlinghetti
          for the rebirth of wonder
and with Whitney Houston
          to exhale.
We waited in deep night to hear
          our son's car in the drive.
We know much about waiting.
European royalty employed ladies
          who did nothing else.
          (Men too, called valets.)
Public space and businesses
          have entire rooms
          dedicated to waiting.
The airport has horrid chairs,
and outside near "Arrivals"
          a pullout lane for waiting.
Waiters live up to their name

at restaurants, though
        now they may be "servers."
Waiting is involved;
We get that, if it's not too long.
We wait anxiously
        for lab results.
We wait in anticipation or dread,
        to be accepted or denied.
Locked out, we wait frustrated
        as if we lost the key.
I get annoyed waiting for you, as
        you are annoyed waiting on me
        and we both have cause.
We are waiting for forgiveness
        for we need it.
We wait for "our ship to come in."
We are waiting for "reality
        to set in."
We know much about waiting.
Might a third way lie between
        assertive Action
        and vulnerable Wait?
Such as only to *Be* – without
        cause or consequence,
        with presence and patience.
There is no requirement
        to simple Being
        but perhaps to free your heart
        to attend to the world –
to linger long in sunlight,
hold a palm out to the rain,
        make space for another.

October 31, 1517

On a quiet Wednesday in Wittenberg
Martin, you took up a hammer and nail
And declaring religion *not* for sale,
Nailed your theses to the door of the church.

Knocking popes and bishops from their perch –
That a priesthood of the faithful would prevail.
Thus went a nascent kirche under sail
Where German faith and commerce converged.

And Martin, what fate from that nail suspends?
It's always troubled me why you would choose
To turn your vitriol against the Jews?
A church door is a small thing to efface.

    But Jesus,
    Whom you love,
    Why then disgrace
To vilify his people and his race.

New Year's Day – When the World Turns

The world turns, revolves.
Nothing to do with anything we did.
We did not earn the new day.
We do not deserve the turning.
It is not the result of our work
or our craft, or our smarts.
It is a gift we cannot change.

The world turns.
God is creating again. Watch out!
We are in the midst of it;
it is in the midst of us.
We are created beings, we are
creation and – what wonder –
become creators as well.

What is the point of New Year's
Resolutions? What is unresolved?
Revolving does no solving.
It is of course a metaphor–
and a metaphor can knock you
down or save you, if you allow it.
We simply draw a line between
a nostalgic past and undiscovered future.

We grant ourselves permission to assign
arbitrary value to a natural process.
The world turns without being asked.
Nothing to do with what we deserve,
only that we give reliable witness to
the inevitability of that graceful turning.

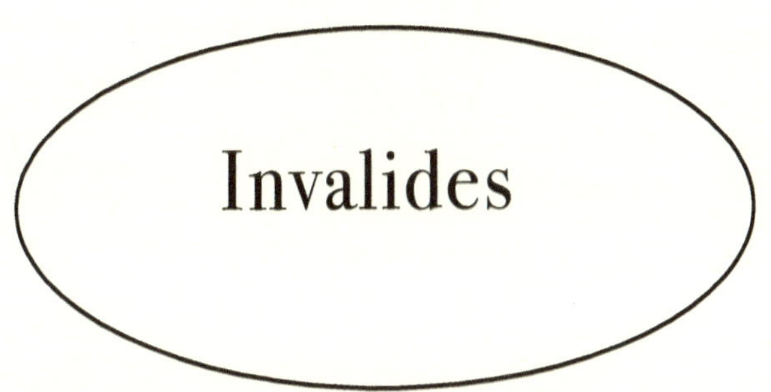

They called again with
reminder of day and time
Give it a rest, Doc

Social Distance

They are not asking us
to come to the rescue,
love one another,
or even be nice…
just to not infect each other.
Seems like a simple request;
but nothing ever is.

Because the young are callow,
and therefore immortal,
the beer'ed and acne'd,
sure they have done nothing
to warrant death,
pack Florida's beaches –
sunburn their only care.

And as if emotion, conviction, and
the certitude of manufactured piety
were inoculation enough,
the pews are crammed.
But faith is not recklessness,
no penance undoes hubris, and
there is no reward for stupid.
Better 6 feet apart than
that same distance under.

Pandemic

(a Pantoum)

We cannot buy our way out of what comes.
The news is on, and every word is death.
From upscale condos down into the slums,
from those with scant, it enters stealing breath.

The news is on, and every word is death,
laying bare our trivial diversions.
From those with scant, it enters and steals breath,
airs racism, dread and mean aversions.

Laying bare our trivial diversions,
ceding to fear all that makes us human,
our racism, dread and cruel aversion,
trump love, community and companions.

We cede to fear all that makes us human,
by Social Distance barred from what we seek –
love, community and our companions.
No antiseptic masks corruption's reek.

By social distance barred from all we seek,
singing "Ashes, ashes, we all fall down."
No antiseptics mask corruption's reek;
impervious to prayer, it wears the crown.

Singing "Ashes, Ashes, we all fall down."
What whimsey passes one and takes the next?
Impervious to prayer, it wears the crown,
and nothing cares for whom it may infect.

What whimsey passes one and takes the next?
Will we still know ourselves? What will we be?
It nothing cares for whom it will infect –
our lives and deaths for all the world to see.

Will we still know ourselves? What will we be?
What trauma will we bear, and then maintain?
Our living and our deaths for all to see,
when gone the virus but the plague remains.

Shelter

(in the epidemic of 2020)

Shelter these days, means "Don't come near."
Don't raise a hand to help, hold or console.
This time our numbers do not make us strong,
and we cannot simply gather any longer.
We must separate if we would be whole.

Yet we lack the discipline of detachment —
are a race unskilled in practicing restraint.
That dread contagion lies in touch or breath,
or companionship may be the cause of death,
runs cross the grain to every way we've trained.

Social creatures need tactile connections.
Though Facebook, YouTube, Skype, Twitter
provided the rehearsal for routines
of "sheltering in place," self-quarantine,
the lack of human touch still comes as bitter.

In streets and walks great emptiness reveals
the smell of absence, the ache of vacancy :
theaters un-played, parks un-recreated,
dates unmade, churches un-congregated.
A dearth of human agency

Shall we study who freely chose seclusion?
How to live in solitude, the sages know.
These I'd offer, were I bidden to suggest
different paths through a life of loneliness —
Julian of Norwich, Hank Williams and Thoreau.

Quarantine

I hungered something like this
when I was seventeen –
that you and I together
would live in quarantine,
high on a mountainside
in a home built with these hands.

An hour and a half below and away
proximity breeds contagion.
City exhaust fuses desert dust,
the virus rages every direction
and death is in each news cycle.
Our mountain fastness may not hold.

But this morning…this morning,
sunlight eases gently in
and we lie, feet locked together.
I feel the softness of your skin
and bury my face in your hair.
Nothing needs to happen ever;
We can stay like this for all time.

Easter Epidemic 2020

Easter breaks in the mountain valley
to *Halleluiahs* anxious and restrained.
Otherwise quiet and still in beauty,
the only sound is the river devotedly
carrying snowmelt down to the fields.

The village is closed to outsiders,
as the Pueblo has already done.
The state highway running through both
engulfed us in solid, heaving traffic
fleeing the city below.

To the traditional affirmation, the faithful
would normally assert, *He is Risen Indeed!*
Online the priest declares, *The Lord is Risen!*
Oh, okay. Good.
I peer into my screen
to see who is still here.

Second Shot

When I felt that second shot
the anxiety abated.
I'll still be distant, wear a mask,
but I'm fully vaccinated.

A neighbor proudly unafraid
owned warnings over-rated,
now lies in hospital with the
very virus she denigrated.

Dogma ardently trumps good sense,
good science is spurned and hated.
No common ground yearns common good.
Just let me be vaccinated!

Why must it always come to this –
a nation contaminated
by discord, deceit and bombast,
and factions alienated?

Hear how hate infects the speech
of hearts grown glaciated.
See rancor wreck and ruin
fondness we once celebrated.

So curse me, call me what you will.
I'm not intimidated.
I'm reviled by the most vicious,
so I'm fully vaccinated.

Virus 2.0

Lauded, he took his pension to
Colorado's Southern Rockies.
His wife found the area,
the nearby town, the fixer-upper
where he would happily turn
his hands to wood and stone.

Retiring to plans for sun, fish,
exploring high country,
he relished the pleasing renewal
with his partner in romance.
Weariness found repair in the solace
and play of a slower pace.

He was doing all this when
the pandemic presented itself
to Montrose County – ever so slowly,
and would it matter?
Vaccinated, remote – for a private man,
life was little changed.

For a time, habitual tasks shored up
their nearly—normal.
When the sole cafe shut down,
the town lost its social network.
The church went digital
and decamped to Vimeo.

Non-profits tried in vain
to plug the gaps, the empty spaces.
Once courted by corporations
for expert innovations,

now he drew the lonely task
of putting canned corn into sacks.

Friends rarely called, nor did he,
but spent too much time with TV,
watching the social contract
devolve to carnival.
Slowly – ever so slowly,
the world receded from him.

The first grandchild was born in Maine,
they could not go to greet her,
and would later miss that instant
where a switch flips, babe to child.
Without ever a positive test,
it was Covid brought him low

The discovered tumor they removed
turned out to be benign,
but internal plumbing started to stutter,
piece by piece in time.
Sympathetic vibration – his systems
failed in concert with the world.

For a time he lived on, struggling
vainly toward gratitude,
the canoe unpaddled, until grief
came and collected him.
The world grew silent;
medical reasons were given their due.

"Crushed beneath a surfeit of despair,"
a young pastor said, daring to deliver
both eulogy and diagnosis.
"He died from an accumulation of loss."

Masking Memory

I'm the only soul in Walmart wearing a mask,
come for want of a critical staple – cat food.
Two years into the epidemic we folded.
Though two-thirds of us are vaccinated,
many will not admit to it, and in the set of
a shoulder or tossing of hair project defiance,
as if stubbornness alone staved off the virus,
as if smug repudiation waved off contagion.
The American Way – pointless bravado.
It might have been better if the CDC had been
less efficient in telling what they knew, and
rolling out theory before they were through.
It might have been better had it not been
politicized, had the Orange Menace not
persuaded his minions the virus was sham.

I load the cat food in the back seat and
lower my mask as I start the truck, aware
the virus still mutates, spins off variants.
In many city hospitals beds are still full,
overworked nurses yet burn out, collapse
and quit – a condition we greet with our best
Scarlett O'Hara – *After all, tomorrow is another day.*
    Souls dying alone,
        un-mourned,
            un-memorialized –
                over a million dead,
and we can't be bothered.
We've been infected in ways we don't realize.

Invalid

The 7th arrondissement of Paris holds
the 17th century Hôtel des Invalides. Today
a museum also, it was created a hospital
for the wounded, the crazed, the legless,
armless veterans of France's bloody wars.
So grandly built, Napoleon chose to rest
with the Invalides to the end of time.
But all things sound sweeter in French.

My own purgatory insignificantly relates –
six months tethered to a catheter,
pain, discomfort, untimely bodily fluids,
surgery that would damn or redeem
and previous experience as an invalid.
In the end the worst is to feel invalid.
Invalid invalid is a complete description
of one who's been too ill too damn long .

Heteronyms – inval´id and in´valid, they
rhyme, spelled the same, but emphasis
changes all when meanings diverge,
when two words stand in a doorway
face to face and stare at each other as if
on reflection mirror images can prevail.
Separāte or separâte, here/hear, feat or feet,
and whether I've become better or bitter?

If I tell you no more than "Napoleon lies,"
have I named him deceased or prevaricator?
We know, for he lies with Les Invalides who,
being deceased, can no longer lie, only lie.
And I have lain an invalid too long abed,

my spirits long since taken leave of me
and fled with what was left of my pride,
closer yet to Napoleon, invalid, in Invalides.

Waiting

Comes now the clipboard Druid to
the court of last resort,
where a line 'tween joy and terror
is just one lab report.

I have learned to hold life lightly
and cherish it far more;
my heart failed back in '92
so I've done this before.

I do not want to ponder death;
I've other things to do.
I've labored under risk for years
and that is nothing new.

…and yet…I feel more fragile now,
in body and in mind.
I own far fewer years ahead
than those that lie behind.

Says the Druid, without drama
(as I am leaning in),
"Negative for carcinoma."
The whole world shifts again,

In a good way. As in "Reprieve."
So quickly it is done,
and then still reaching for belief,
I walk out in the sun.

This time.

Dying Re-considered

If I say I am afraid of death
        I mean yours.
I've been rattling on with two-thirds
of a heart since Prague in '92.

But absent of you, the old
generator is sure to throw a belt.
        You're who keeps my heart,
the only one who knows the fix.

Taxidermy is an option, but
grandkids don't need a shabby
        stuffed Gan-Gan substitute
molding away in the corner

I love you, but don't want to outlive you.
And you are the practical one.
I drink too much and wax blue, am more
        prone to go out roaring.

I do *not* choose to spend my last days
        lying in my own urine,
smelling it all day, in a
featureless "care facility."

Alternatively, how about being
        shot to death by Federales,
while I smash up a bar in Caborca?

I bought two burial plots today,
anticipating our demise.
        Framed between two great boulders,

with a pine-treed view.
Not that we'll ever use them, or care,
when we're gone. Some future genealogist
may find they help fill in some blanks.
            Just don't go without me.

Borderline

Her keys collected; she gathered her belongings,
      carried them alone out to her big black Ford.
On Monday we will turn on the lights
      and start over.
There will be no notice, no severance,
      only an emptiness.
The pills let her live within
      her life's margins,
until too many and too often
      took away the lines.
In the Breakroom they made bets –
      sunshine or thunderstorm.
She may charm the world one moment with
      bright and dimpled smile,
and be the next crouched in the corner looking
      up from under perfect bangs,
eyes turned dark and hard as anthracite
      save diamond pinpoints of rage.
Would the trim professional stride in
      briskly and with confidence,
or would it be the sullen shuffle of
      matted hair and sallow cheeks?
Who flies from fine to fucked-up
      in five seconds flat?
One job to the next, one love to another, she
      responds to impulse,
afraid of being present and afraid
      of being left.
The female Mantis plots murder
      as she plots romance.

She may have lost her margins, but I have
          not lost mine.
Headed north on I-65,
          in another hour the black Ford
will cross over
          into Kentucky.

Losing My Mind

The brain seems vulnerable.
Stress, trauma, certainly head injury.
Would it not have been better
to spread things out a bit?
A glob in the abdomen,
a bit in the left thigh, and so on.
Holographic. The current arrangement
seems to contain a design flaw.

It is the brain where we keep our minds, yes?
Our language betrays our fear, our anxiety,
that what goes on behind our eyelids
may not be normal, is cognitively impaired.
Are we fixated on losing our minds?
"I will lose my mind if I hear that song one more time!"
"That kid is driving me out of my mind!"
"This program just makes me crazy!"

We have invented so many ways to lose our minds:
flip out, go ape, freak out, crack up, break down,
go crazy or –a serious one – lose your marbles.
Don't wanna do that. Keep food on the brain,
and go nuts, be bananas, a vegetable,
two spring rolls shy of a #5.
So much language. We are deft and daft about this.
Lose your mind in a good way, be over-enthused,
crazy in love, mad about the girl, be a holy fool.

When she does something risky, rash or wild,
if he hears voices, has recurring nightmares,
when she is erratic, when he has mood swings,
when he is exasperated and she is frustrated,

he/she may be on the way to losing their mind.
Will they disassociate, enter a fugue state, go psycho?
Should we check for tumors? And why is it
I can lose my mind, as they say,
but never seem to find it?

The TV says the mind is a terrible thing to waste.
On the flip side, we see the smartest minds as
dangerous – sharp as a tack, a mind like a trap,
can be a pistol or (in a malaphor) is smart as a whip.
But my tribe, aging boomers, struggles to recall names,
afraid we will be swept into the dementia epidemic.
Parents with Alzheimer's lose their minds,
and we fear for ours. It would be a terrible last stop
on the Mystery Tour.

––––––––––––––––

This is a stupid poem.
A more-than-stupid poem
There is a reason for this.

Tonight I puked my brains out
in the wake of indigestion, gas and rumbling discontent.
I am not drunk; I am not sick.
Some other cause must be assigned.

People more commonly say they "puked their *guts* out".
When you puke your guts out, unattractive
odors are generally involved, off colors,
perhaps some solids and unassimilated food.

The expectoration in question tonight, though,
is clear and viscous – the consistency of
protoplasm, or hair gel.

I think I puked my *brains* out, because on examination,
suspended in the gelatinous medium
were threads of philosophy and bits of doggerel,
recollection of a picnic last summer,
memories of a broken heart from years past.
Thrown up and done, down the drain they go.
I worry that entire sonnets have been lost.

Here it comes again, abdominal muscles clenching.
There goes Minneapolis, and the recipe for paella.
I'd hate to lose Addis Ababa.
I always wanted to visit that place.
And what's the name of that band
that sang "Penny Lane"?

There is certain indignity to find yourself
puking your brains out in the lavatory
of the men's room at Fuddrucker's.
I know what you're thinking.
Who hasn't done *that*? Nonetheless....

Brains rhymes with grains, trading b for g, rains
with neither. Scramble the letters – pains, feigns,
cranes. Many rhymes for brains, but maybe
not for long when you are losing your mind.

The woman who lives in my house
(what is her name?) thinks this process

has been underway for years.
Maybe thirty of them. Who knows?

There are advantages in puking your brains out.
One could lose....
- Daytime TV
- Facebook
- Dallas Cowboys fans.

Ugghhhh…there goes the capitol of Kentucky,
and all my French.
What's the name of the team
that plays in Wrigley Field?

Time to stop this.
Where is the woman who lives in my house?
"Honey, where do we keep the Club Soda?"

There are *dis*advantages to puking your brains out.
It is no consolation that bad memories,
even negative programming, can be
lost along with other content.

For one thing, I have grown from pain, sometimes.
For another, how can I take consolation in
what is not there? How would I know?
And would I always wonder?

———————————

In my old age, I am losing my mind.
I think that's good.
It's a sign of maturity.

122

To mind is to care – care about or care for.
The older I get the less I mind.
What is it they say?
"Not my circus, not my monkeys."
Healthy differentiation.

Mind your manners,
mind your P's and Q's?
At my age I'm not minding
my goddamn P's and Q's.
Better advice – mind your own business

In high school I minded very much
what Kristi thought, and thought of *me*.
I worked up nerve to ask, "Can I kiss you?"
She fluttered her eyelashes,
smiled coyly, and said, "I don't mind."
"Well forget it then."

The state of Colorado doesn't mind
if you use recreational marijuana.
Massachusetts doesn't mind, and
neither do I. I lost any mind about it.
Just don't drive into my lane.

I moved to Alabama;
they said I had to pick a team,
Alabama or Auburn? And
I couldn't do that because
I don't mind. I really don't.

I have not lost my mind when people's rights
are abridged. If they (whoever they *is*)
do it to others, they can do it to you, or to me.

I mind less these days –
pretty much lost any mind I had.
I am narrowing down the mind-able list.

I do mind about the things that matter:
Poetry, music, truth, justice, friends and family,
fine whisky and a good, good woman.
Did I miss anything that matters, really?

Space

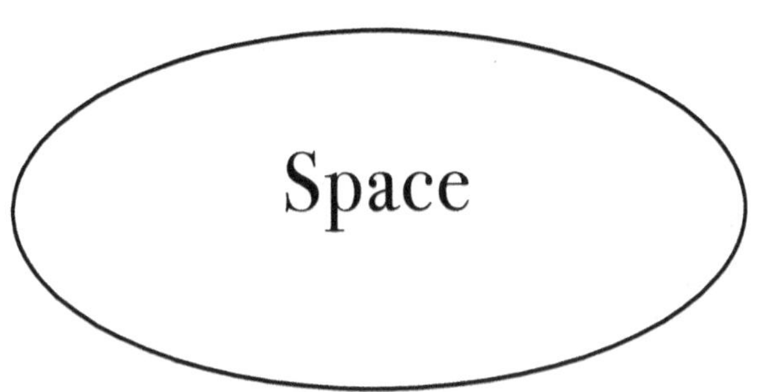

Up there is nothing
than whatever will be here
just lots more of it

Perseid

The cat is curious I'm not abed.
Cold footed out on the deck, staring up,
this elevation above the dust layer,
at a velvet sky jamfrosted with stars.
Nearer suns and planets boldly-dressed,
Aldebaran and the orange one is Mars.

A bright rising moon floods heavens above.
and most details gave way to its glory.
As the cat has his snack, a meteor
flies cross the grain to all other light.
Fifteen meteors, three cars and a plane
in an hour – a ratio about right.

Look long enough and you understand how
the ancients, who named constellations,
could lie awake on their backs for hours
gazing into the depths, wondering why
mere flesh is gifted with reason to ask:
How vast is it all and how small am I?

Sated, the cat retires down the hall.
Seems gravity-bound meteors trek endless void,
yet just one of them killed all those dinosaurs!
Space debris, asteroid, meteor – called all.
99 bottles of beer and if
one of those bottles should happen to fall…

Conjunctions – 6:20 am

Venus and Jupiter in conjunction;
Mars in attendance is wondering what
in the universe gave her compunction
to bunk with so burly a brute.

Mars has matters of his own to manage.
A UAE ship entering orbit won't land,
and so promises less damage than
Chinese and US Rovers behind that will.

Dawn; Venus demurs, so Jupiter's gone.
Mars still steams from insult imagined when
a voice says in Arabic, as if on cue,
"Red planet in the corner pocket."

Mars Advances

High drama out at 4 AM.
This chance may be my last;
it will not be this big again
until 15 years have passed.

Mars has commandeered the sky –
bold, orange and formidable.
The neighbor we've been calling on
continues inhospitable.

To my right, the Roman god of war;
on my left the Greeks' great hunter,
Orion with his Dog Star trailing,
through a sky awash in wonder.

A bright half-moon attends the scene –
brave Luna with a running start
makes encampment in between,
to keep those war-like boys apart.

Still, red Mars glows as if he bleeds,
as close to us as he can come,
to retire the field and now recede.
… What if he doesn't? …

The System, By Jove!

Who gets to name the planets?[1]
And why do not the sods
relieve us of the detritus
of Greek and Roman gods?
Did Ptolemy so cleverly
choose distant lights that move
as deities who'd leave us be
and stay at safe remove?

John Glenn flew high and so began
an off-of-this-world race.
Now there's Branson and Bezos,
the first billionaires in space.
Planets no longer seem so far,
even when the trek takes years.
We've sent out probes and so
we know we can get there from here.

Bare Mercury too near the sun,
beauty of Venus storied and sung,
and the goddess of love as well,
must be why she's the hottest one.
Home, in seven hundred languages –
Terra, Gaia, Eretz, Arde,
in English just a throaty grunt
that could near-rhyme with dirt.

Mars, our second closest neighbor,
where all the crawly Rovers are,
may soon unveil a Martian diner,
or possibly a Mars bar.
Biggest Jupiter, Boss of gods,

we sent your love, Juno, out where
she found within your atmosphere
sprites and elves live there.
Flashy Saturn, with your 82 moons
and a thousand rings so fine.
I won't talk about Uranus,
if you won't speak of mine.

Neptune, blue and icy-far,
is this the sea for which you strove?
Or half-forgotten where you are?
Would you rather be by Jove?

Pluto. Is it planet or no?
Or does it sound like years ago –
when Blacks were two-thirds of a person
("demographic purposes," you know)?
The orb has its own five moons,
with Charon, Hydra, Mickey and Nix.)
So it's a "Dwarf Planet" now, with
Kerberos, Sneezy, Sleepy and Styx.
      Given all this, should we not
      the advent of a new age prove,
      and set out to rename the lot
      for classic Rock and Roll, by Jove?

Freddie, Bananarama, Wind and Fire,
Bruno, Springsteen, Ringo,
 (but enough about Uranus),
Pharrell, Little Richard

Pythagoras saw conjunctions
of the planets' light and sound.
His math was true, right angles on,
and all his worlds were round.
Rare harmonies, that old Greek stored,
they resounded in his ears.
So, is voice or an open power chord
the music of the spheres?

[1] The International Astronomical Union

The I.S.S.

Celts were already in long migration
when they fled into Gaul and Anglia
with Roman Legions in pursuit.
So much deemed exploration was
sourced by survival or sired by greed;
we call it history now.

The International Space Station explores,
experiments and measures, not for
fear or acquisition, but to Know.
Aboard the I.S.S. today they are studying
the effects of microgravity on muscle mass,
and detecting algae blooms in the seas.

My grandson leads me into the wondrous
reedy wetlands behind his north Jersey home
in our endless search for PeterPan
(as if one word, accent on first syllable).
Armed with plastic swords and imagination,
we brave to travel where others turn aside.

The I.S.S. 250 miles up, orbits the whole earth
in 90 minutes, racing steadily across the sky,
17 and a half thousand mph, far above
the atmosphere, so far yet so close. I can see it
for 6 minutes only, this pass – a startling bright
mercurial teardrop! There are people in there!

An old woman's feet slip into faded pink mules.
She shuffles slow down the produce aisle,
then stops, remembering the taste of corn.
A woman self-named Yggdrasill throws a leg

over the Harley seat, wrapping arms around his
jacketed back. Gothic script reads "Lost Boys".

The I.S.S. has hosted 250 astronauts from
20 countries since 1998. Different cultures,
races and genders work together. Our world is
conflicted by the interests of nations.
What could we learn if we simply looked up?
Water purification methods, medical advances.

1958 – TNO Rail hauled freight Houston to the Gulf,
behind my house. Ellis and I put pennies on the track.
Flattened coins made us luminaries at school. Wizards.
The young woman with worry lines,
shifts her baby from one arm to the next,
and struggles to open the car door.

Our I.S.S. annual cost equals 1½ B2 bombers.
In billions, our war budget is $750. Discovery is $22.
There are practical things that need funding.
How many killer drones could we build for that
kind of money? Has anyone run the numbers?
Remind me what it is we get for that expenditure.

The Station is presently crewed by 7 diverse people
of 4 nations. Can we be becoming better people ?
As he ascended Jesus said, "Now don't follow, y'all."
Or something like that. We didn't listen. We never do.
So why space? We're from Narnia, and Middle Earth.
And well…maybe, just maybe, we'll find Peter Pan.

UFO Breakdown

In 1947 when the craft went down
there was major commotion all over town.

They brought in pieces of the thing at risk
along with the pilots of the flying disc.

A nurse walked in and said: "My stars!
What you got on the table is a man from Mars!"

The Air Force gathered up the evidence and
locked it at Walker AFB, behind a big fence.

They flew it to Ohio on the very next day,
but I swear I overheard a G-man say:

"Someone in Roswell knows
what happened to the UFO's!"

The local paper reported this crime,
and it got picked up by the London Times.

They rounded up the Rancher who broke the news
in New Mexico, and corralled him for an interview.

He said: "That's the dumbest thing that I never seen.
(Pssst. Oh, and by the way…they ain't green!")

Without a saucer, and missing a corpse,
people just went on back to work, of course.

Everybody went about their day to day,
but every once in awhile you'd hear a local say,

"Someone in Roswell knows
what happened to the UFOs!"

Ever since the UFO came that day
there are things unexplainable in some other way:

Edsels, body-piercing , hoverboards, Pet Rocks,
the Pot-bellied pig craze, Twitter and Crocs,

global warming, Tucker Carlson, TV-wrestling.
Don't forget Grenada and bucking machines.

Things are getting stranger every day,
and I have an idea how it got this way.

But try to get the files on the flying disk
and the GAO will tell you that they don't exist.

Someone in Washington knows
what happens to the UFOs!

I was riding the swing out late one night
when there came upon me a blinding light.

I've seen strange sights on the range, of course,
but it was all that I could do just to sit my horse.

I can take the flashing lights, don't mind the rattle,
but it makes me nervous what they do to the cattle.

On solitary nights beneath a prairie moon
I get the sense that I'm not alone.

I do feel better about the human race,
knowing there's a back-up in outer space.

Someone in Andromeda knows
what happened to the UFOs!

Heartsong

Naked to morning
outside the tent she stretches long
Maybe showing off?

Oblation

Wake slowly into stillness
so silent ears ring seeking referent.
This day no engine startles from the road below,
no snarling chain saw rattles the canyon walls.
This day no stalking wind finds the pines;
Piñon and Ponderosa stand silent sentinels.
The dogs lie dumb and dormant.
The elastic cat stretches and recoils
ever so slow back into position.
A dove calls a single comment and falls mute.

There come those rare and gentle days of
tranquility and calm. Soon the Woman will stir,
and soft from the kitchen will come muffled
sound, the clink of a spoon on a mug's edge.
We will share unhurried the coffee sacrament,
and rise into a holy Saturday blessed by
dearth of demand, absence of obligation.
There come those consecrated days of the
purity of being, the grace of simplicity.
Be still, and know…

Colorado

The novelty of intimacy,
more than any real affection,
lured two teens into a mountain dream.
In the middle of that great silence.
I kissed her in the wilderness,
and held her arm through a crystal stream.
The mist turned cold to a gentle rain.
We sheltered 'neath a fallen fir,
we laughed when it soaked our backs again.
We touched, and all the world was her.

The thing is, we could not make it last
and what goes up need come back down.
I tried to reclaim that place and time
but it was never again the same.
I'd conjure up her limpid eyes,
the face and lips I would paint with rhyme,
and the fading blush of afterglow,
there on her brow the dampened curl.
Truth, I loved rain in Colorado
more than I ever loved the girl.

Bold Chicago, tall, gritty, complex.
And she, so lovely that it hurt,
that her scarred arms screamed her pain.
Intimacy with that novelty
found me deep in those wounded arms.
Then she left. I never saw her again.
I can't shake the memory of her bed,
how long that damaged touch would stay.
I loved a Blues guitar on Halstead
and let the woman slip away.

As I look back now with seasoned heart,
She shines like gold in middle Fall.
She has loved me fierce through health and pain
everywhere – through two dozen nations
and through twice that many autumns,
sun in Panama or Prague in rain.
Intimacy of familiarity
grants comfort and the freedom to,
with all passion, joy and clarity,
love the woman, not the venue.

Heart In a Field

"Somebody Left a Heart in a Field in Ohio
Now Police Can't Figure Out Where It Came From."
                     Washington Post, September 19, 2016

A human heart in an Ohio field;
No one knows where it came from. (But I do.)
It's not even decomposed, they revealed.
(Yet I suspect it was broken in two.)

I once left my heart in San Francisco,
Seriously. And twice in Santa Fe.
But deny love at night in a meadow
And all your secrets expose you in day.

You can give up your heart to a lover.
You can surrender wholehearted to God.
But a heart all alone in the clover,
Bound to naught, is decidedly odd.

I would bet all the sera hematose
That somewhere there is a woman who knows.

Hester

Pen Pals in our early teens,
Australia was a world away.
Her letters postmarked *Sydney*
bore exotic stamps. I kept them.

On the leading edge of puberty
I harbored erotic thoughts.
Laughing, fair and lovely in my mind,
she chased kangaroos, cuddled koalas
in the Outback. Her on the beach,
bare skin bronzed and dripping.

'What-if?' lingered, a whim she might be
mousey and frail, lost in an insipid life.
We sent no pictures, so the only
curator was a fertile imagination –
the safest place to secrete reality.
Long-distance love was not long lasting.
She was no steadier a scribe than I.

It would never happen today.
It is nothing special so nobody does it.
No more exotic stamps of kangaroos;
the Internet put an end to that.
Lives and photos are there for the taking.
No pen pals, no imagination required.

What interest would I have held
for her anyhow – an oil-field brat
stuck in a dusty high-desert town
between mesa and mountain,
deep forest and the Navajo nation?

Strictly No Touching

Strictly No Touching, the signs all declared.
I was 21 and randy;
She was 22 and bare –
for all of east El Paso to enjoy –
wearing nothing but a G-string and a smile.

I drank my beer as slowly
as the bouncer would allow,
to stretch my cash
for tips that bought her time.

She was barely shy of pretty
and a mediocre dancer,
but her breasts were things of wonder
to a boy of 21.
High, tender and firm, they trembled
when she walked, and so did I.

On break she sat cross-legged
on a stage direct before me,
while all of time and reason stopped.
Perhaps there was what passed
for conversation, I scarce remember,
as her foot slipped toward me
underneath the rail.

Beer-fueled brave, I moved my hand
to cup her dusty sole with my palm,
stunned and thankful she did not cry out,
nor jerk her foot away,
nor signal the 300 lb. gorilla in the blue tux.

She stared into my face
while my eyes fell to her chest
and that pair of soft white rabbits
quivering just out of reach.
I gently rubbed her toes,
for a very long time (or until break was over).

We made a date to meet at 8
the evening following,
where I returned to learn
it's her night off.
She wasn't there. She never came.
From the vantage point of 40 years,
the memory of her bosom fades;
but still her toes, her toes
are titillating.

Ode to Black John

A grad school friend up north who
I hadn't heard or seen in months,
phoned. I left Santa Fe, he Forth Worth
and we met in El Paso to drink.
By "El Paso" I mean Juarez.

Not real Juarez, which is not a bad town,
but the infamous border strip where
you drink up one street, the next go down,
through lights, music, strippers, tequila,
and young Yanquis gone to get stupid .

Our cash fell low, we should've gone back,
but an adverse notion arose –
we'd win it all back at the Juarez dog track.
We just had to pick that right hound,
put it all on one roll and go safely home.

We cased kennels of dogs waiting to run –
lean, rangy bodies of quivering energy.
Ten minutes more and I saw the one,
tall and muscled, his name was Black John.
His green silks bore number 4.

I read of John's stellar track record, though
I placed the bet with some caution yet.
I picked the black dog to Win, Place or Show,
a safe wager was sure to yield something.
Confident, we returned to the stands.

A mechanical rabbit sped round the track.
In rapid Spanish the announcer chattered

owner, breeder, stats – each dog's extract,
then in English as the hare tripped the gate,
"Heeeere comes da bunny!"

Every new race, Greyhounds run for their
lives, which tend to be ugly and short.
One loss too many they're buried out there,
their bones given over to desert.
It's a dog's life.

I spotted John near the head of the pack,
amid narrow heads stretched for the lure.
They hit the straight, I turned to look back
at the screen to be sure of the finish.
Number 4...finished fourth.

I woke in an alley just off the street,
thanking the gods of the Aztecs.
Someone not me had pissed on my feet,
still I had my flat wallet and keys.
An hour later I found my truck.
My friend made it on home but I'd taken a yen,
as I left Mexico for South Texas,
at Grandma's ranch she'd sure take me in.
My earliest years were spent there;
we neither of us ever forgot.

When Grandfather died she took a career,
the first social worker in Texas,
at the Gainesville School for Boys for years.
Then she went back to the ranch
where her heart was.

I got there and worked two weeks beside her,
thirsty for talk, vaxxing goats, pulling wire.
Then for hours at night before we'd retire
she'd tell stories that I'd never heard,
about the golden olden times.

She gave me hundreds in folding money
on the morning that I had to go,
her usual smile between tough and sunny.
What I didn't know was I'd be the last family
to see her alive.

More than two hundred miles up the trail,
something pestered and poked at my mind.
I suddenly realized I had failed
to record a single one of those stories.
I pulled off the road and cried.

So number 4 Black John, here's to you
on the day your legs let down your heart.
Loser of Stories, here's to me too
and the tears in my heart that won't dry.
We almost got it right.

A Cruel Rain

The sun was crowded by
a rain-dark cloud.
Juniper and sage, rabbit-brush,
thrust up thirsty branches,
thinking to break their fast.
Rain fell in a gray sheet,
visible for fifty miles as
long lines descending
in the dry air and arid heat.
It vanished, vaporized. Virga
that never touched earth,
it offered only hope
and proffered only dust.

Like that one day in El Paso
where I stood on the assigned corner,
my head filled with her,
my heart filled with her.
Feeling ever more worry
as time passed, I held my post.
I waited long, 137 minutes,
before I left.

Sacrament

There are verities known to women
they will not tell to men, so I
continue unoriginal in my sin.

Not the Body of Christ, but hers
is desired, the pristine sacrament –
 redolent in scent, sight, and touch.

Desire finds merely her curved back,
her gentle slumber unencumbered.
My supplication falls soundless.

The selfishness of the sacrifice
that longs for even one soul to see
and tell my tale, proves its impurity.

To an empty temple I return, the
waste of Un-sculpted *Davids*, unsung
habaneras, half-written *Hallelujahs.*

As always, my offering is Cain's;
no one is there to receive the gift.
I hurl a prayer into the dark heart of God.

MamaRuth

was a compound word in East Texas.
I knew her best as a sentient vegetable,
and have no remembered conversation
with my maternal Grandmother.

Day-long in a high-backed cushioned chair
she sat imperious, impassive, a royal mannequin
passed around the family like high-value artwork
that no one bid on.

MamaRuth had forty-six treatments of
electroshock therapy between '47 and '63.
MamaRuth had checked out
when Mom got polio at 10 and had to
raise her little sister and brother.

When she did come to stay awhile,
she would appear mid-morning
after great preparation to sit silent,
unmoved and unmoving
in an aromatic cloud of eau de toilette.

Mom said that MamaRuth came
to help after Dad's heart attack.
She did not. She was in a locked ward
in Dallas. The dates are on the microfilm.

Mom said MamaRuth came to help
when I was born. She did not.
Mom so craved a mother of her own,
she invented one.

When Wilbur Went

no one cried.
Or maybe they did,
    maybe they tried,
    not that I remember.
Am I imagining, or was that
    up and over trip to
    East Texas, about not
    grief, but obligation?

I was 5 years old and
    I didn't know what
    "dead" meant.
I sure do now.
There's a lot what's dead –
    possibility
    promises
    chances
    choices
    bonds
    bards
    heroes and hopes
    mentors
    memory
    and at my age, friends.

But when Wilbur died,
    no one wept,
as I remember.
 So why did it take me
    fifty years to learn
    that my Grandaddy
was a sorry drunk?

Things We Can't Un-See

Abecedarian

Among the wounds inside we
Bear are old memories we
Can't un-see. Example: the
Day I took the ring back, her
Eyes were dry, but rage aged her
Face twenty years in seconds.
Gone the laughing girl, and in
Her stead a hard woman set
In. There're things we can't un-see.
Just wall off the memory.
Kids with rocks throw at troops who
Looking, hunting, aim and fire –
Mostly echo noise, save a
Nine-year-old who lies face down
On the street, pink dress wicking
Piss and blood and mud in the
Quiet that follows such things.
Ray, who is my age, had a
Stroke that rendered him just a
Turnip. Mournful things we can't
Un-see – his glassy blue eyes
Vacant and roaming, and the
Watery drool from his lips.
X-rays, MRI's, etc. – then can
You un-see *you* in the Time
Zone of the living dead?

Verdure

Soon the last tower would fall, and his new place
took more greenbacks but promised safe and clean.
One last time Irlandés pulled his van away
from that shame the Southside called Cabrini-Green.

From the speakers Rev. Al sang *Take Me to the River.*
With ice ahead he eased up to the stoplight.
He missed water and liked Lake Michigan,
so when the light turned green he took a right.

Chicago was no colder than his tropic home was hot.
For half a year no green was to be found.
Far too many rats, too few frogs and lizards,
and everywhere the grass and trees were brown.

Grass is always greener where you're not,
his dreams were colored emerald, jade and lime.
Young and yet untried, he was determined –
deliveries were income when he got there on time.

A woman-child at home, baby on the way,
at lunch he turned the I-90 form in to renew
his green card at Citizenship and Immigration.
That done, hungry to the grocer then,

for what she liked – frozen pot pies, vegetables,
bags of green tea, ham with mayonnaise,
and the cheapest Vinho Verde to be had, that
they could use to lift a glass to better days.

The speakers in the van pumped music –
I Hope You Had the Time of Your Life.

When he made a little more he would save more,
then the woman-child could be his wife.

He took one last pleasure before heading home –
      the van he'd park at Navy Pier and
      walk its length over water
      to peer intently into
      the dark at an
      illusory small
      green
      light.

Women's Crew 8+

Long bare arms in the sunshine,
their oars reach for the sweep.
Eight blades together slice water
to the count of the cockswain's call.

Long bare legs in the sunshine
together thrust the sliding seats
back and forth in perfect time,
shoving the shell to the finish line.

2,000 meters, robust row-or-bust, and
eight young women fold face to their oars.
Limbs tremble, sweaty chests heave for air.
Who could not adore them?

Yada

"Adam knew his wife," old King James said;
it took me forty years to understand.
In scornful youth, I thought the religious
just too prudish for vernacular –
screwed, fucked or copulated. But No.

Yada, yada, yada, the summary
skips particulars, and loses meaning.
Hebrew, *yada,* to know – as nuanced
in an ancient tongue as in this one.
Adam knew his wife, and so he did.

Know, meet, understand, get, grok, perceive,
have intercourse with, and covenant.
Experience, discern, see, feel, *yada.*
Adam knew his wife in all the ways.
God knew Moses, and no one thought it queer.

Adam knew his wife, and so do I.
Over forty years my field of study –
I've a Master's in her satin skin,
and a Ph.D. in her smooth flesh,
and pondered long on places she can't see.

She rocks up on her toes when eager,
and tucks a wisp of hair behind her ear,
and scratches her scalp after orgasm,
a "tell" she doesn't know and wouldn't own.
If Adam knew his wife, he's not alone.

How strange to know a body better
than I can ever see or know my own –

the new mole on her inside forearm
with not one, not three, but two soft hairs.
Adam knew his wife; he paid attention.

Adam knew his wife, it says. I know.
The lipoma which will not leave her back,
each ridge on the old C-section scar –
holy line from navel down to glory,
grace in every blemish, line and scar.

If I find morning in her laughter,
in her eyes the deeps, in her hands kindness,
forgive me if I love her more than God.
"Adam knew his wife," old King James said.
Yada, yada, yada. I know, I know.

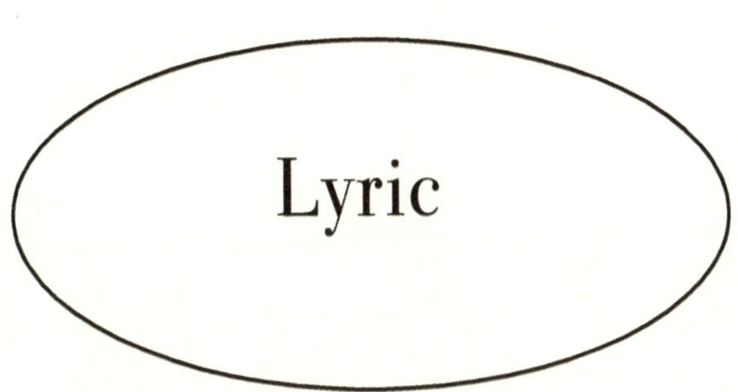

What difference lies
twixt a lyric and a poem?
Call it what you will.

Unlikely Way to Glory

Sitting Bull wasn't born to war.
He was a faith hero, a medicine man,
caring for his people
when the white men took the land.
Neither Lakota nor Cheyenne could foresee
>how a simple country preacher
>could wipe out the 7th Cavalry.
But how the mighty fall,
there is no way to know
how the man who took down Custer
ended up in Cody's Wild West Show,
>riding round the ring
>in feathers, shooting 6-guns.
>Sitting Bull is that now your story?
>Cops killed you on the Rez in 1890
>Just to keep you quiet, old Ghost Dancer.
It's an unlikely way to glory.

Mary Rugg poured coffee
at a truck stop on I-10,
and if you've come into El Paso
from the east you might've been there.
She called the drivers all by name
and knew the rigs they drove.
>For 20 years she brought 'em eggs
>and hash browns from the stove.
"Best waitress in the city,"
the Times said in '83.
She took the news by phone, said "Thanks"
and turned around to pour iced tea
>for 30 more years
>of her laughter and her tears.

When she died they didn't make another story.
Some truckers pulled their cabs around
and shone their lights out on the ground.
That was about it.
It's an unlikely way to glory.

We would not have heard,
but for the spoke or written word,
of Sitting Bull's or Mary's lives.
Take another look
because every life's a book, and
God bless the poets and the scribes.

Ever since time began
we've told tales by the fire.
Whose kill-shot got the mastodon,
and who's the biggest liar?
Maybe it's that light and warmth
will make creation spark.
Or that outside of that circle,
there are dangers in the dark.
Someone's got go;
Leave that to me.
I'll go out there and take a look,
come back and tell you what I see,
because now I'm getting older,
I'm not much use for else;
I'll just sing my songs and tell my stories.
Maybe when I'm gone,
There'll be someone come along
and do something with them. Probably not.
It's an unlikely way to glory.

Heart of the Stone

Walk down by the river
        where the mountain sheds its tears,
and the water's carved a channel
        over seven million years,
cutting through the topsoil to the bone;
its passage there is
        written in the stone.

Where it's worn the rock away,
        there underneath is shown
the fossils that are evidence
        of when the world was young,
creatures that were here and now are gone –
the record of their living kept
        forever in the stone.

Which is stronger, solid rock
        or the water's constant force?
The banks may be eroded,
                still they hold the river's course.
Underneath the stream that's rolling on,
secrets of the ancient world
        are hidden in the stone.

The Anasazi built the first
        great cities we found here.
They made their homes at Chaco
        and again at Bandelier.
From the land itself their lives were grown,
where the ancients broke their
        hands and hearts on stone.

It's only guesswork why they came
        and where they are today,
or why they left their houses,
        homes and fields and went away.
Who can answer where and why they've gone,
when most of what they left us is
        a puzzle writ in stone?

The rock is smooth to touch,
        the workmanship is fine.
The walls may sag in places,
        still they hold the builder's line.
Within these ruins somehow souls live on
with secrets of the ancients hidden
        deep within the stone.

At Stonehenge and Callanish,
        the circled stones you see
are standing up on their hind legs
        to point to mystery.
All that proofs and arguments have shown
is that words don't have the
        half-life of a stone.

A plain and simple slab of rock
        like most you ever saw,
in the hands of Michelangelo
            becomes the Pieta`.
Rock and brick and mortar, much the same,
with crafted skill and prayer
        becomes a Notre Dame.

The piece that's chipped and cracked was
          once precisely planned,
though damaged and discolored still
          can show the sculptor's hand.
It still remains here when that hand is gone –
the secret life of humans hidden
          deep within the stone.

Some say that I'm a hard man;
          is there emotion under there?
Is it true I've got a heart of stone
          or just that I don't care?
Maybe they would find it harder too,
if they'd done some of the
          things I've had to do.

Fill up your life with vanities,
          belabor plans and schemes.
Just hope you're tied to solid rock
          that's deeper than your dreams.
You'll wake one day to find your choices gone,
and learn that time was passing
          as you set your work in stone.

It's only striking steel that
          causes flint to spark,
and the heart that has been broken
          still can bear the Maker's mark.
What could have been still will be unknown,
and the tears that otherwise I'd cry
          are hidden in the stone.

One More Bronc

Spent last night in Memphis,
hung the sign 'Do Not Disturb,'
Now it's fill the tank and shoot the bull
with the boys who ride the curb.
Tomorrow night in Birmingham
it's the arena once again —
about as east as I have ever been.

I've been riding rough stock
from the day I turned sixteen,
local shows and sometimes
well-head pumpjacks in between.
When I made the circuit I was
riding with the best,
and put my old-time skills
up to the test.

One more serving of instant nerve
and I'll be good to go.
I'll climb back on again.
I got one more bronc left in me.

Everywhere I go, I've got
songs inside my head,
they play all the time,
wherever I get led.
I don't mind the company;
it's a way of keeping track
of who I am and why,
and how I can get back.

But nights are getting' longer
and I'm not as strong as then,
and the one who waits and loves me
wonders when it all will end.
Falls I took when I was young
hurt days just like they should;
now they hurt for months,
or hurt for good.

But just four pills of pharmaceutical will
and I'll be good to go;
I'll climb back on again.
I got one more bronc left in me.

Was it about the ponies or
was it about the lights?
Or the life I might've had
if different choices worked out right?
It was poetry in motion,
pure horse-dance till you're thrown.
Now it's time to pack it up
and go on home.

There comes a point the thrill is gone
and everything's the same;
nothing in the repetition
tells you why you came.
No one tells you how much
Rodeo is about the road,
or how lonesome life out
on that road can be.

One more day of make-believe brave
and I'll be good to go.
Then I won't do that again.
I've only got one bronc left in me.

In the morning I'll turn the truck
the other way around,
put the rising sun in my rear view
as I drive out of town,
and listen to the radio
while the miles just fall away.
Turn left at Colorado,
I won't stop till Santa Fe.

Who Will Remember?

Hey, what happened? Here we sit,
       wingtips on our feet,
       saying "Sir" at someone half our age.
If I could, I'd get life's remote and press repeat,
back to the time when we held center stage.

I remember a Saturday
       in nineteen seventy-one,
       when you rode Sidewinder for eight.
King of the cowboys, you were a reckless sonofagun
but you'd shine when they opened up that gate.

Here I am, going through
       my drawer for collar stays;
       it takes longer now for me to look my best.
What those are, where they come from, I can't say,
but I need all the help that I can get.

But when I'd unpack my guitar
       at the Red Garter Saloon, those
       springtime cowgirls took the sawdust floor.
I sang pain and truth to steel guitar and a prairie moon.
They'd smile at me and always ask for more.

In my prime I was in demand,
       there was a time
       before everything I wrote went out of print.
I'd take vagaries of life and make them rhyme;
now my CDs go for 97 cents.

I wasn't there at Woodstock, when
          Neil Young sang a warning
          that the Age of Aquarius would be late.
But I still like the smell of tear gas in the morning,
like Chicago in 1968.

Where did the time go by?
          We meant to change the world
          together, you and I.
We aren't getting' any younger, that's for sure,
          but who will remember what we were?

New Orleans 2005

Down in the bayou where the Mississippi winds
where Creole and Cajun come together, in the minds
of the people there's a piece of Voodoo magic called
the New Orleans.
It's a righteous party, get your dancing shoes.
Join the nuns and hookers on a riverboat cruise;
the temperature is rising,
down in the New Orleans.

An oyster Po' Boy on a summer's night,
drinking Dixie and Abita till you get just right.
Fetch you some Tabasco from the shelf
and get some more red beans.
She gave us gumbo and etouffee,
does anybody care she's washing away?
The waters are rising down in the New Orleans

Neville Brothers, Connick, Hirt and Domino,
Gatemouth, Cowboy Mouth, Dr. John and Satchmo,
the music's always rising from
down in the New Orleans.
Jazz and Blues and Rock and Zydeco,
now the Black and Blue musicians have
no place to go and the silence of the city
is an empty and an eerie thing

The water's coming through at 17th Street –
Cat 4 storm's got all the levees beat.
It won't be long before the dirty water's
coming through the screen.
It's gonna wash the dead folk outa their graves.
All the poor folk on the housetops are

begging to be saved,
and calling to America,
"Won't someone help the New Orleans?"

Comin' up on a Gulf Coast hurricane,
screaming winds like you never seen
were pushing up death and danger
from the Pontchartrain. Up comes the water,
down in the New Orleans.
Why did so many people have to die?
Out there in the dark I heard a baby cry.
Can they hear it up in Washington?
Won't someone help the New Orleans?

Oban Bay

There's a tower unfinished on the hill above town,
what McCaig meant the point to be, I couldn't say.
Let the mind make of it just what it will,
each time I return it is standing there still,
keeping watch over Oban Bay.

Down below they make whisky, and make it so fine
you can open the bottle and smell the salt spray.
Soaked up from the sea by the peat on the hills,
it flavors the water that runs down in rills
and mingles in Oban Bay.

The last time I came I had loved ones with me,
now I'm by myself at the edge of the quay,
where my daughter stared, with the wind in her hair,
across the water to Mull, and wondered what's there
on the far side of Oban Bay.

Just at the tide change the harbor draws breath,
and one shaft of sunlight reaches the wave.
A lone piper tunes up and skirls in the morn.
The town comes alive to the ferry's great horn
at daybreak on Oban Bay.

The fishermen sort out their lines and their nets,
on the sweet scent of diesel they motor away.
Seagulls go wheeling up into the sky,
their hopes taking wing on the wind, so do I
in the sunrise on Oban Bay.

Slow Train

I gave up my seat when he got on at Calais,
because he said he was a refugee.
He was stooped and bald; he said he spoke Spanish
but he sounded pretty English to me.
So I bummed him spare change and
we shared half a sandwich
and I listened to his story for free.
Then he drifted away to sleeping again,
and I went back to just riding the train

We sat back fine, buying wine from the trolley,
rolling south out of the Gare de Lyon.
In the parking lot below
a man was heisting a Mercedes,
breaking in a car that wasn't his own.
He had professional tools, and he wasn't in a hurry;
he grinned as we went gliding along.
Then he turned away, hey whadda ya say?
There are just some days its gonna happen anyway.

Two young boys about to get into trouble
as Chalon sur Saonne came into sight.
They were stuffing big rocks in a long pair of socks
and swinging them with all their might.
We worried their intentions and
we worried about the windows,
everybody gauging distance and height
till with a shout of joy it all came plain
as the sock-rocks went flying over the train.

She got off the train when we pulled into Macon,
disembarking she's the only one.
She trailed a scent of lavender, walking down the quai.
The station boys were holding their tongues.
She was tall and lean, quite
clearly a thoroughbred,
but not above enjoying some fun
because she tossed her long hair, and blew me a kiss.
Hey, I like riding on a train like this…

The thing about a train is it doesn't need explaining.
I sit back and ease my mind.
All that needs knowing is wherever I am going
is whatever there is waiting at the end of the line.
I like a slow train, so I can see what's coming.
On a slow train, I can tell where I've been
and smile while I'm looking out the window,
waving back at the people who are looking in.

Anywhere But Here

He left the job at noon and he didn't go back
to the work he'd done for 25 years.
He said, "After everything I put in here,
I don't have to listen to this."

    With his heart growing hard
    he went and sat in the yard,
    with an open half a bottle of beer.
    He thought about throwing out
     a piece of his life,
    but not before he made him a list:

of all the unpaid overtime, late nights and weekends;
smiling faces, all full of pretense –
playing their emotional corporate games,
all looking for someone to blame…

    He thought "If I could be anywhere but here,
    point the hood of the car at the morning star
    till I'm anywhere that isn't here."

She looked at the clock and reflected on the man
she's been married to for 21 years,
and wondered why they say that it's better this way
than a woman just living alone.
    But she won't start crying
    while she's still trying
    not to realize the worst of her fears –
    will he hit someone again
    if he bothers
    to even come home?

So she wanders the house making everything all right,
takin' care of every little thing that might start a fight.
Just about the time the deck is clear,
on her face she feels a tear.

        She said "If I was any old where but here,
        I'd take the rolling wheels of an automobile
        and the wind in my hair and how that feels."

He sat under the trees with his head in his hands
looking older than his 33 years.
Waiting for security forces to take him,
he wasn't going to put up a fight.
        But he wasn't too proud,
        so he talked out loud,
        and he didn't care if anyone hears.
        "If I could have just one good
        friend to help me make it
        through a dangerous night.

But from the start now I've been on my own;
it's come down to me and me alone.
What's going to be will be at last,
but if I could I'd let this cup pass.
        If I was just anywhere but here.
        I'd take a rolling stone on a distant hill,
        a long time alone and how that feels.

If I'm up at dawn I could be long gone
before anybody sheds a tear.
If I could be anywhere but here."

The Artist

(for Fred Wise)

The Artist takes a brush in hand
       and has a stab at life.
Sometimes he gets it wrong;
       sometimes he gets it right.
Sometimes he gets his heart broke,
       and his pocketbook broke too,
to bring those pretty pictures home to you.
They say Monet had a better way
       of representing light,
but I've been watching haystacks,
       and I don't think that's right.
I think he painted shadows
       in the places light forgot,
to show what was by where the light was not.
       Dali stretched the fabric,
       of very space and time,
       and left it draped upon
       the bare trunk of our lives.
       He knew the way we looked upon the world
       was only hampered by our eyes.
Allori paints the angel
       that's bent to Mary's ear,
who whispers bold epiphanies
       she doesn't want to hear.
We who watch are caught
       by something greater than the frame.
Who sees that whisper never is the same.

So Wise recalls New Mexico,
        and pops another beer,
and asks the empty canvas,
        "What am I doing here?",
then paints *Golden Girl and Saxophone*,
        alone without a band,
with colored wands that stung and scored the hand.
        What's the color of heartache, and
        What's the proper hue to use
        for hunger in the night?
        If I played all the shades of blue
        in C# minor would it
        help to get it right?
        O'Keefe painted just one scene
        about a hundred times –
        in different ways the mountain that she loved.
        She said that God had promised it to her
        if she just painted it enough.
When Woody paints the forest lakes
        they fade into the mist.
What else lies there behind the fog,
        we're only left to guess.
And what lies in the Artist's heart
        is something you can't name,
you only get to see what's in the frame.
The Artist takes a brush in hand
        and has a swipe at God.
The poet does the same with words,
        so I don't find it odd
to show the master painter
        the shadow in your soul.
Who put it there's the One who ought to know.

If I Wake Up

You know we're all going to die;
One thing everybody has in common.
There is no reason to cry;
It's not like we didn't see it coming.
       Cancel your appointments, let it end;
       Then it's life and death and life again.
We stumble, fall and rise just to keep our place.
I don't think much about death.
There are other things I have to do today.
But I hold you closer than breath,
So the tide won't wash us away.
       But if you let go of you, and I let go of me,
       Our rivers will all run together into the sea
And I'll never have to live without your embrace.
I've always wanted to fly –
Like it's the next stage of being human.
You know we're all going to die,
And it's not like we didn't see it coming.
       There's a time for loving, and letting go –
       Not the easiest thing, I know.
When the time comes, let me fold with a little grace.
At the end of all things, there is a gift:
Life and death come as a set,
And we'd never die if we had never lived.
Coming closer every day if we're not there yet…
       The days go by, then the years go by.
       I can't slow them down
       no matter how hard I try.
But if I wake up in the morning…
       Let me wake up in New Mexico
       Looking for your beautiful face.

Author Bio

J. Shannon Webster grew up in the Four Corners
area of New Mexico, playing songs for short cash.
His several hats include: community organizer, pastor,
musician, lecturer and frequent workshop leader.
Recipient of NAACP Alabama's Community Service
Award, he was recognized by President Obama
for his social justice work in Birmingham. Author
of too many papers, articles, and manuals, he also
released three independent albums of original songs,
most recently recording in Muscle Shoals. He is
published in three anthologies: *The Social Distance,
Poems for Hungry Minds,* and the New Mexico Poetry
Anthology 2023. He lives with wife Lou Ann
in northern New Mexico.

An independent publishing company
dedicated to bringing the printed poetry,
fiction, and non-fiction of musicians who
want to add to the power and reach
of their important voices.

www.ingramcontent.com/pod-product-compliance
Lightning Source LLC
Chambersburg PA
CBHW031040160726
47991CB00005B/1963